Be Where Your Feet Are

Be Where Your Feet Are

Seven Principles
to Keep You Present, Grounded, and Thriving

Scott M. O'Neil

with Randal A. Wright
and Michele Bender

ST. MARTIN'S
ESSENTIALS
NEW YORK

Published in the United States by St. Martin's Essentials, an
imprint of St. Martin's Publishing Group

www.stmartins.com

Designed by Steven Seighman

The Library of Congress cataloged the hardcover
edition as follows:

Names: O'Neil, Scott M., author.
Title: Be where your feet are : seven principles to keep you present,
  grounded, and thriving / Scott M. O'Neil ; with Randal Wright and
  Michele Bender.
Description: First edition. | New York : St. Martin's Essentials, [2021] |
  Includes index. |
Identifiers: LCCN 2020056318 | ISBN 9781250769879 (hardcover) |
  ISBN 9781250769886 (ebook)
Subjects: LCSH: Conduct of life. | Values. | Success.
Classification: LCC BJ1589 .O54 2021 | DDC 170/.44—dc23
LC record available at https://lccn.loc.gov/2020056318

ISBN 978-1-250-85269-4

Our books may be purchased in bulk for promotional,
educational, or business use. Please contact your local bookseller
or the Macmillan Corporate and Premium Sales Department
at 1-800-221-7945, extension 5442, or by email at
MacmillanSpecialMarkets@macmillan.com.

First St. Martin's Essentials Trade Paperback Edition: 2022

10 9 7 6 5 4 3 2 1

*To Lisa, the love of my life, my strength,
my comfort, and my everything.*

*To Alexa for your strong will, to Kira for your
compassionate heart, and to Eliza for your loving soul.
Thank you for making my life complete. I will root
for you forever, love you for all eternity, and be there
for you for anything, anytime.*

*To the leaders, managers, teachers, coaches, moms,
and dads who choose to inspire, love, and develop the
next generation of amazing people—thank you, the
world needs you now more than ever.*

Contents

Be Where Your Feet Are

Introduction

Being challenged in life is inevitable;
being defeated is optional.
—Roger Crawford

"This is the last time you will ever speak to your daughter. Tell her everything she needs to know for the rest of her life. You will have an hour with her, make it count." I was at Camp Joy in the backwoods of Ohio with Kira, then 11 years old, on a Young Presidents' Organization (YPO) retreat for fathers and their preteen daughters. There was a child psychologist facilitating this exercise for the CEOs, and as I looked around, everyone seemed as wide-eyed as I was. The task felt daunting—especially after hearing we would have just 30 minutes to prepare. I grabbed a piece of paper and scribbled some notes, but my head was swirling. It wasn't making sense. Actually, I wasn't making sense. *Wait, this isn't really the last time I am going to see her, right?* I thought. *But, what if it were? Why isn't this easier? Why haven't I had this conversation already? What am I waiting for?*

Thoughts were still rushing through my head, with nothing usable or even legible written on the scrap of paper that I had tucked into my pocket, when I met up with Kira. But once we started walking, I felt a sense of calm as we strolled hand in hand, with the only sound being the leaves crunching under our feet.

We walked for several minutes before I began. "There are three things I want you to know. The first is family, family, family. Friends are terrific, but they come and go in your life. Boyfriends are fleeting. On-line connections are just that. But our family of five is forever. Love more, lean in, lean on, and cherish our bonds. Focus on how you can contribute as well as draw strength from these connections. There is nothing more important than our family, always and forever." Kira squeezed my hand tightly as she heard my voice cracking.

"Second, it will always be okay."

"What will be okay, Dad?" she asked, looking up into my eyes and smiling.

"Well, things, a lot of things will go badly from time to time, and at that moment it will seem like you're facing the biggest unclimbable mountain in the world. But, it isn't."

"The mountain?" she asked. I laughed.

"Yes, the mountain can be a lot of things, Kira. You will fail a test. Friends will disappoint you. You will get detention. There will be breakups. Someone close to you will die. You will lose a big game. You will make a mistake. You will fail at something. You will be laughed at by a group of mean girls who then bully you online. You will crash your car [this one was actually a bit prophetic]. There will be a period in your life where you feel like you're alone and nobody is listening to you or helping you. But no matter what it is, how tough it gets, or how deep you are in that valley, know that it will *always* be okay. You will always be okay. It *will* get better. The sun will come up the next day. You have to know that it will always be okay." I took a deep breath.

"Third, anything, anytime," I said, feeling more confident.

"What does that mean?" my 11-year-old asked sincerely.

"Anything, anytime. I am here for you. You can count on me. You can call me, text me, FaceTime me, and I will be there. I am here for you. I hope to be a sense of comfort, a reality check, a loving shoulder, a support system, and the person you can call when you need to laugh or cry. I will listen. I will not judge. I will only love. You are never alone. I love you forever and a day."

That walk established an unbreakable foundation of

a relationship between Kira and me, and we continue to build on it today, many years later.

What's most important (or WMI, as we call it at work)? Yes, that was the question for me, and that is the question for you. This walk and talk taught me a valuable lesson: life doesn't stop and allow you to say what you feel when the world is swirling and moving so fast. Most of us don't have the time—or is it that most of us simply choose not to take the time?—to share WMI, what we are thinking, and what we appreciate in others. We need to do more of it, and you will when you choose to be where your feet are.

That is one of the positives that came out of the COVID-19 pandemic in 2020. It was mostly negative, too many deaths, too much pain, and more struggle than seemed reasonable. However, it forced us to check ourselves, slow down, and even to pause time and space to reflect on the lives we were leading. I started this book before the pandemic, but the time I gained from it would reteach me its lessons in ways that I wouldn't have thought possible in the rush of everyday life. In the months that followed, which were the beginning of the pandemic lockdown, my wife, three daughters, and I painted, played board games, puzzled, did dribbling drills in the kitchen, baked, ate meals together, had movie nights and cleaning parties, read, and went for family walks . . . all things that didn't seem to find their way into our lives before the pause. One night we had "bring your favorite stuffed animal to dinner." Another night it was "color war," where we each dressed head to toe in our favorite hue. The things happening in our home had never happened. This is not a real-life version of *The Brady Bunch* or other perfect TV family, of course, as we experienced our fair share of the emotion, arguments, and disagreements that come with three strong daughters. But we received the gift of time and space, and ever since, I've been trying to engage the message sent and the lessons learned to make my life more meaningful.

What helps pull it all together so these takeaways materialize? Making the most of each moment and ridding ourselves of the toxic habit of constantly looking forward to the next thing. *Be where your feet are.* But how? For me, it has come not only from finding the lessons in my own experience but also in listening to other people's stories. The result has been better relationships at home, stronger leadership at work, and feeling more engaged in my community.

I was motivated to write this book because I was exhausted from having people ask how to find balance in their work and personal lives. It is a popular ethos that never made sense to me—the idea that we should all seek "balance" is bad misdirection and often leads to failure on all fronts. The problem with this concept of balance is that it has us aspiring to a mediocre middle.

Being present, focused, committed, and hardworking at home and at work is the path to finding success and fulfillment.

I am at my best when I am locked in where my feet are. That is to say, I'm 100 percent present and focused wherever I am at any given moment. This is not always easy for me, and it is a work in progress for all of us, but I am trying. My goal in writing this book is to start you on a lifelong journey of self-discovery toward reflection, action, and fulfillment.

The stories told in *Be Where Your Feet Are* provide an array of tragic, uplifting, and inspiring anecdotes that oftentimes were inflection points in the storytellers' lives, moving them in a direction they would have found unthinkable until circumstances forced change upon them. Fortunately, if we open our minds and our hearts and embrace the lessons learned, the stories will teach us and inspire us and we will have an opportunity to thrive in the parts of life that really matter.

As you might imagine, a fair share of the stories come from the sports world (hey, that *is* my day job, as CEO of the Philadelphia 76ers and New Jersey Devils), but there are also plenty about life, love, and learning coming from a dad, a husband, a middle school girls' basketball coach, a mentor to young men at church, a son, a brother, and a friend. This intersection of life, work, faith, relationships, struggle, and triumph plays out in this collection of moments, memories, and experiences wrapped up in a thing called life. It is important, though, that each moment (good or bad) provides us an opportunity to learn, and if we choose to take it, that opportunity can change our lives, and the world, for the better. This is something that took me decades to understand and appreciate, and it is what we tried to capture in *Be Where Your Feet Are*. If you get just one nugget of insight or inspiration that helps you live a more present or grounded life, then this book has achieved its goal. So let's get started . . .

CHAPTER I

Be Where Your Feet Are

If you must look back, do so forgivingly.
If you must look forward, do so prayerfully.
However, the wisest thing you can do is to be
present in the present. Gratefully.
—Maya Angelou

Pause for a minute and consider the environment in which we live. The pulse of the world is dictated by sensationalism and efficiency. And noise. Too much noise, all the time.

We race and rush through our days. We compress our thoughts into 280 characters. We demand the antibiotic over the phone without seeing the doctor. We spend hours filtering our lives to wrinkleless perfection—no generation in human history has cared more about people "liking" them. We now curate our own media, providing polarizing views to complex issues that are summarized in a few sentences—specifically designed to grab attention. This pushes us to the edges of the middle and often beyond. Sensationalism sells, and all of this online mess manages to enrage, further divide, and bring a sort of energy and extremism to our world that we'd be better off without.

Our minds lack focus and travel with a speed equal to that of our lives. For those who are hard-charging, ambitious, and on the rise in their careers or other endeavors they're passionate about, the line between work and home and home and work has blurred to the point of disintegration. We are always "on," accessible and available.

With so many distractions, it is harder today than ever to be where your feet are. It has also never been more important. It is unlikely you will ever find me teaching at a Zen meditation center, as I don't always do a great job of finding inner peace or feeling content with simply "being." That's just not my natural state, although sometimes I wish it were. When speaking in front of groups, big and small, I'm always asked versions of the following questions about balance: Can you be successful at work and have a good home life? If you want to be a great dad, can you succeed at work? Can working moms have it all? How do you find work-life balance? My answer is always the same: I have no idea.

It is not because I don't work a lot; I do. It is not because I am not connected and at one with my family; I am. Nor is it because I am happily tucked into my chair at the dinner table at 5:15 p.m. It is not because I don't put a high priority on my wife, Lisa, and my daughters and my career; I do. I simply have no clue in this day and age how to find work-life balance, and that is more than okay with me. It is okay because it is not the answer I am concerned about, it is the question . . . it is the wrong question. I don't believe the good life is about finding balance between work and home. It's about living the moments we have *where and when we have them*. Balance does not breed greatness, and as my good friend Lara O'Connor Hodgson is fond of saying, it is not much fun to play on a see-saw that is perfectly balanced.

The question we need to be asking and answering is: How do you maintain the discipline to be where your feet are?

When I'm at my best, I am wholly present. When I'm at work, I'm at work. When I'm with my kids, I'm with my kids. When I'm coaching the seventh-grade girls' basketball team, I'm totally there, in the gym. On a date night with Lisa, I am 100 percent present. Of course, no matter how much I want it to be true, I'm *not* always at my best. On occasion, Lisa has told me, in her own way, to put my phone down. "I'll wait," she'll say, and then stare me down. Translation: "If you think that text you are reading is more important than our time together, please let me know, and when you are ready to have a meaningful conversation, I am ready." Hearing her say that never feels great, but it is better than the message I am sending her with my phone in hand, eyes down, and ferociously typing. So, no, I am not perfect, but I aspire to continue to improve and work toward a more present me, because I am better at all aspects of life that matter when I am in that space.

And so are you.

Being present is harder than ever. For all the goodness and increased productivity that 24/7, readily accessible information and connectivity have brought, they have made compartmentalizing roles, jobs, and responsibilities tougher and tougher. There is no longer a start or stop time in the workday. Instead, we can walk on the treadmill while scrolling through a presentation, listen to voicemails on line at the grocery store, and check texts in the middle of the night (or worse, while driving—please don't). Movie theaters have to actually run ads during the previews telling us we cannot text during the main feature!

We have a problem. We need to be more present.

Here's a four-part process to help this journey:

1. Find perspective;
2. Seek authentic feedback;
3. Cultivate reflective strength;
4. Live your leadership constitution.

Find Perspective
The Blue Duffel Bag

My 76ers colleague Dave Sholler, our executive vice president of communications, embodies the ability to be where your feet are. He is famous in our office both for his inspiring commitment to his family *and* for his ability to remain remarkably focused when work requires it. He is known for saying, "I am going to have to call you back in 15 minutes, playing games with the kids," or "I have to call you later, our family dinner is about to start." But when it comes to high-stress moments where the communications department is on the front lines—the NBA draft, free agency, a big trade, or simply a team struggling to meet lofty expectations—Dave shines. He defuses incredibly tense meetings with an easy smile, a reassuring comment, and his unique ability to direct people back to the core point of the meeting when it has gone astray. What keeps Dave grounded and has made him the person he is today and fuels his mindset and priorities was a life-altering experience that happened more than 25 years ago.

Dave grew up in a trailer park just outside of Atlantic City with his mother, his three younger siblings, and his on-again, off-again dad, who had battled drug and alcohol addiction for as long as anyone could remember. His father was in and out of every sort of rehabilitation program—inpatient, outpatient, faith-based, non-faith-based—but nothing seemed to work and, as a result, he put his wife and children in an ever-worsening series of difficult situations.

"My dad was a very fun and charismatic guy when he was sober," Dave explains. "He was the same way after the first drink or hit, but by the second or third, the monster came out." Dave was ten years old the day his school bus pulled up to his family's trailer just as a police officer escorted his dad out the front door. Without looking in Dave's direction, his dad suddenly pulled free, grabbed a bike, and cruised right past the school bus and out of the neighborhood. Dave's mom, at her wit's end with his substance abuse, had called the police.

For a while, his father lived under the boardwalk and then made his way to a homeless shelter. Believing maybe this time he would stay clean and determined to try to keep their family together, Dave's mom agreed to pick him up when the shelter called her.

"It seemed like we had done the drive to rehab facilities and shelters a million times, but I'll never forget *that* day," Dave explains. It was one of those crisp, cold winter mornings where the wind off the Atlantic Ocean cuts right through you. The type of weather where you just want to stay home under the covers. But Dave's mom loaded her young children into their old, beat-up Chevy van that his dad had gotten as payment in exchange for some plumbing work years earlier. "There was my sister, who was eight, my brother

Danny, who was three years old, and then my youngest brother, Dennis, who was a baby laughing in his car seat. I remember wishing I was like Dennis: too young to know what was happening and oblivious to where we were heading," Dave recalls.

As the old van limped down the highway toward the shelter, Dave felt his anger rise by the mile. "I thought, why do we live in a trailer park when all our friends have backyards and rollerblades and all that stuff? I was tired of the eviction notices and wondering if every knock at the door was someone telling us it was time to go. I was tired of the expression on the cashier's face when our family paid with food stamps and the condescending looks from people at the welfare office because my mom was there with four kids under the age of ten," he says. "I had already grown up too fast and learned too much from the school of hard knocks, but I was about to get my PhD in perspective from that same school."

As they pulled up to the Atlantic City Rescue Mission, Dave saw a young woman standing on the steps with three children about the same ages as Dave and his siblings. He immediately recognized the expressions on the kids' faces: shame, anger, tension, and the here-we-go-again look. When Dave got out of the car and walked closer to them, he saw that they were carrying their belongings. They were not at the mission to pick up a troubled dad; they were going to stay there themselves. Observing the forlorn mom, lugging a raggedy blue duffel bag, and her bone-tired children, Dave suddenly realized: *We could have it a lot worse.* The family on the steps didn't have a van. They didn't have a trailer to sleep in at night, and they probably didn't have the baseball glove Dave's grandfather had given him. Everything in their lives was in that blue duffel bag. Everything.

"I think about that moment often, and it pulls me back," Dave says. "It reminds me that some of the 'problems' I have today are minuscule compared to what many other people are going through. That blue duffel bag also affects the way my family moves forward today. My wife, children, and I are big supporters of that same rescue mission, and every year at back-to-school time, Thanksgiving, and Christmas, we reach out to them to find families going through what we did. We live 5.7 miles from the trailer park where I grew up, and I recently took my seven-year-old daughters to see it. I want them to have a level of perspective about where I came from and gratitude about where they are now.

"It's important to me to raise appreciative kids and to cherish every moment I have with them."

★ Grounding Principle ★

About a year ago, one of Dave's daughters asked him the toughest question ever: "How come you don't have a dad?" (He and his father are estranged.) "Being able to think on my toes is part of my job in communications, but I wasn't ready for that curveball," Dave explains. "Yet, I went back and told her the story of the blue duffel bag, but in a way I never had before because my lens had changed. That blue duffel bag was a source of strength for me at a time when I needed it most. That blue duffel bag is not only about perspective, but also about gratitude and hope. I talked to my daughter about how fortunate we are to have so many incredible people in our lives and the power of perspective."

The Good Old Days Are Today

Don Jabro and I met at Harvard Business School. During our first conversation, he told me he was going to be a hedge fund manager, and I pretended I knew what that was. Fast forward 20-plus years and Don Jabro, in fact, fulfilled his goal at Shellback Capital. Recently, while we were talking about life, work, parenting, and being where your feet are, he shared an experience that had stopped him in his tracks (and gave me pause too). He was out to breakfast with his young son, Graham, on a Saturday morning. It was a rare moment when just the two of them got to hang out—his two daughters were at a sleepover, and his wife had an appointment. Curious about a postgame press conference following an exciting college basketball game the night before, Don was searching on his phone for what the losing coach had to say after the stunning upset.

As he was eating and watching the press conference, Don noticed an elderly couple at a nearby table looking in his direction and grimacing. A few minutes later, the couple finished their meal, got up from their table, and left the restaurant, or so Don thought. Two minutes later, the woman came back to Don's table and, without saying a word or making eye contact, placed a note scribbled on a napkin in front of him. Then she turned and hurriedly walked away.

"You should pay attention to your son instead of your phone. You only get this time once," the note said.

★ Grounding Principle ★

"My initial reaction was anger—what do they even know about me? Are they implying that I'm a bad dad? How do they know that I didn't spend the entire morning with Graham, and this was the first time I looked at my phone?" Don says. "I was tempted to go make my case to the woman, but then reality set in, as did the pit in my stomach: she was dead right. It's so rare that I get to spend quality time alone with my son, and I wasted it watching a senseless sports video instead of just talking to him. Since that day, every time I have the chance to have private time with any of my three children, I remember that note and either turn off my phone or leave it in the car. If I am fortunate enough to see that couple again, I will thank them, because they truly changed my relationship with my kids. This special time *will* be gone in a flash, and I don't want to look back someday and think I wasted it." *Perspective is the foundation on which we build a life where we can be where our feet are.*

Seek Authentic Feedback
Garden of Dreams?

Both Dave's and Don's stories have helped me too, and so has some blunt feedback that Lisa once gave me after I came home in a particularly salty mood one night after yet another Knicks loss. (I worked for Madison Square Garden Sports years before becoming CEO of the Sixers.) I wanted some understanding and maybe even some sympathy, but Lisa quickly put me on my heels.

"How good are your teams?" she asked, referring to the New York Knicks (NBA), New York Rangers (NHL), and New York Liberty (WNBA), all of which were going through rebuilds. Before I could answer, Lisa continued: "With three losing teams, I'm projecting over a hundred losses this year. Is that about right?" I nodded my head sheepishly, thinking through each of the teams, the upcoming schedule, and the mounting losses. Her not-so-subtle point was crystal clear: I was working 150 or so nights a year. Family time was precious—our girls needed their dad, and she needed her partner. So, if one out of every three nights at home was going to be a woe-is-me-I-need-some-space pity party . . . it was not going to work. She was right, of course. I had a choice, and her lecture provided much-needed perspective, a reality check. The status quo wasn't working for me or her.

I made it a practice to get everything out of my system before I walked into the house each night—a practice that I continue today. The moment I open the car door upon arriving home has become a kind of prompt—that action sends a signal to my brain that my feet are entering a new zone. My job at that moment is to be present for my family and not let the day's stress or a tough loss impact my time at home. I recommend you create your own prompt. Maybe it's hanging up your coat and taking off your shoes. Maybe it's tossing your keys by the front door or powering down your cell phone. You might even put up a sign that you'll see immediately: You are now home. Be where your feet are!

Ready, Aim, Get Fired

Losing your job will test you, push you to the limit, and teach you even more when and if you are open and willing to learn. The emotions that often accompany it—shame, guilt, disappointment, self-doubt, a feeling of being untethered and alone—can cause you to spiral downward. It can also reveal who your true friends are and provide profound learning moments (if you can shake off the bad feelings). It was one such experience that taught me a lesson central to this chapter.

I got fired from my then–dream job as president of Madison Square Garden Sports. It was a very public firing—the kind that makes you feel like you'll never recover. On that very day, my friend and mentor Peter Guber, the former chairman of Sony Pictures who now runs Mandalay Entertainment and is one of the controlling partners of the Golden State Warriors, the Los Angeles Dodgers, and the Los Angeles Football Club (LAFC), came to see me and gave me some life-changing advice.

Peter had, coincidentally, also seen me on my first day of work at Madison Square Garden, the World's Most Famous Arena. That first-day conversation went something like this:

"Scott, how long are you going to be here?" he asked.

"Forever," I replied without a moment's hesitation. After all, I was a New York kid who was now president of the sports group of the incomparable Madison Square Garden. Forever seemed realistic.

"Scott, I'm being serious," he said.

"So am I. I make a great living, I get to play basketball on the Knicks' court. I am surrounded by the titans of New York business, sports, media, and entertainment. And, we are spinning off to be a separately traded public company. We are putting $1 billion into the arena to carry on the legacy. This is the center of sports and entertainment in the world. I'm never leaving."

"You know what you're saying, right?" he said.

"Am I being naive?"

"You could say that," he replied.

"Okay. Maybe ten years? Twenty years?" I said a little less confidently.

"Look. Just leverage this platform and create meaningful relationships. Use your skills and take advantage of the incredible size, scale, and opportunity. Make your mark on this city and this organization."

Fast forward to my last day, which came just a hair earlier than forever. (Four years, actually.) I was in my office packing when in came Peter, who happened to be in the city for the day and had heard the news.

Avoiding pleasantries, he dove right in. "I've been through this before," he said, referring to his very public firing from Sony Pictures. "Here's my advice: don't let your Type A crazy take over."

After looking me directly in the eye to make sure I was hearing him, he continued.

"You're going to have the urge to prove everybody wrong and prove how smart you are, how hard you work, how driven you are, and how connected you are." He paused. "By the way, we already know that. You'll want to have a job in eight minutes and have this big press conference to show the world that you can bounce back. Don't. Fight off your instincts. Just shut it down. Take time and space," he said. "Go decompress. That's the first step."

"The first step in what?" I asked.

"Just find a beach somewhere, bring Lisa, and tuck

that phone away. Get the *you* back in you. Get the life back in your eyes. Find yourself. Then call me."

I took in Peter's words, but man, it was hard to do what he advised. It was a very insecure, fragile time. Oftentimes your job becomes a large part of your identity. When you lose that job, you don't know who you are anymore. And this can make the most basic of human interactions a nightmare.

Shortly after the firing, I was at the drop-off line at my daughters' school when I saw the twentysomething carpool monitor.

"Scott, what are you doing here?" she asked.

"Uh, um, just dropping off the girls. I mean, you know, just, well, okay. See you." I felt the heat run up from my toes to my forehead as I nearly broke into a sweat.

Minutes later, I caved in my commitment to taking time off. I called a friend, Dan Singer, at McKinsey.

"I need a consulting project," I told him.

"Really? I thought you were taking time off," he said.

"No."

This was about creating an identity—more like a security blanket—so that if someone—anyone, actually—asked, "What are you doing?" I could say that I was working on a consulting project with McKinsey. People "explore other opportunities" all the time, but I wasn't okay saying, "It didn't work out," or "I'm checking around," or "I'm just taking some time off." I was

so banged up that I couldn't even say, "I'm good without a job." I didn't realize it in the moment, of course,
but that was a real window into the fragility of life and
the human ego.

Fortunately, as I hung up the phone, Peter Guber's
words ran through my mind. Peter is a seriously wise
man who has given me more than my share of spot-on
advice over the years. He was right: it was time to let
go and decompress. My psyche was so banged up.

Three days later, Lisa's mom and dad flew in from
Utah to stay with our girls, and she and I went to Cabo
and checked into Las Ventanas, which is still my favorite resort in the world, for ten days. Despite me being a
near total disaster of a travel mate until about day three
of the trip, I was able to snap out of it. My phone never
left my room. I read a bunch of books (eight of them).
I took long walks on the beach, ate delicious food (way
too much of it), and saw some incredible sunsets, all the
while connecting with Lisa in a way we hadn't been
able to for years. We talked about our life, our dreams,
and our daughters. We smiled a lot and laughed a ton.

Two days after we got home, we pulled our girls out of
school to go to Europe. (The first time I was out of work,
after running a startup into the ground—which you'll
read about later—I was dead flat broke, not a nickel to
my name, and I couldn't pay our mortgage. Not so fun.
This experience was a little better thanks to the sever-
ance you get when you're fired from a high-profile job.)

We went to Paris and London for two and a half weeks, a trip that my daughters will say was the best of their lives. Why? Why was it so good? Was it the hotels? The Eiffel Tower? Tower Bridge? Buckingham Palace? No! How could that be the best *ever* for them? Because I was 100 percent where my feet were. For the first time in my life, I had nobody to get back to—no "quick" emails to dash off or "short" phone calls to take in the middle of lunch. I was so free that when we were at Euro Disney for my youngest daughter Eliza's sixth birthday, I was singing the Gaston song from *Beauty and the Beast*: "Now that I'm grown I eat five dozen eggs, so I'm roughly the size of a baaarrrrggge." I was doing it loudly, so loudly in fact that I caught the attention of the Disney employee dressed as Gaston, who, not so politely but well in character, turned around and yelled, "Shut up!!!!" Eliza was mortified and still says it was the most embarrassing moment in her life. If you are ever unlucky enough to hear me sing, I apologize, but it does give you a sense of how relaxed, carefree, and comfortable I was becoming.

I'm not a big museumgoer or sightseer, but we toured. We walked and held hands. We posed for selfies. We ate. We hugged. It was an incredible time for all of us. (That was despite the truancy notices we got for the girls. I wrote in one email response to the school that "spending time at the Louvre was more impactful for my kindergartener than coloring." I thought this response was not only true but also hysterically funny. Lisa did *not* think it was funny. Not at all.)

★ Grounding Principle ★

It was this incredible time when I was actually fully connected to the world, myself, and my wife, kids, and friends. I was interested, curious, reading, and learning again. I was seeing things differently. Somewhere on the train between Paris and London, I had a "Why not now?" moment. Why can't I have this connectedness all the time? Why can't I always have this sense of awareness and fun? It hit me: *How you live is truly a choice. What you're going to do and who you are going to do it with, those are choices only you can make.* That was my "aha" moment.

Wake-up calls—we *all* get them, from bosses, from spouses, from partners, from friends, but for those of us who are parents, the ones involving our kids can hit the hardest. Seek out feedback from those who love you enough to give it to you (honestly), and if what you hear does not match the expectations you have for yourself . . . change! And, yes, sometimes the gift of feedback arrives in the most unexpected and timely way, like it did for me. But the lesson for all of us is: Lower your screen. Eliminate notifications that draw your attention to your phone. Take your texts off vibrate. Eliminate two social media apps. Leave your phone in the car when you go out with your children and have them do the same. *Be where your feet are more often, and life will be better and more fulfilling.*

Cultivate Reflective Strength
Me, Meditate? Ah, No. Well . . . Maybe?

I will not urge you to slow down, because I love the speed of life, as my good friend Karen Hung calls it. I will warn, however, that sometimes we rush through it at the expense of actually living it. It's a subtle but important distinction, and one at the very heart of being where your feet are.

I was 39 years old when my mother, concerned by what she observed to be an increasing strain in my voice and life, introduced me to an executive coach, Tricia Naddaff. My mother spent a career working with executives from ADP, Xerox, McDonald's, Texaco, and others, and she knew the sound of someone struggling. It was 2009, and the world was upside down from the financial crisis. I was in the middle of an aggressive culture change plan, and Madison Square Garden was about to embark on the most ambitious $1 billion-plus arena transformation in sports history. I was all over the place that year: at times every bit excited, lonely, ambitious, cautious, happy, anxious, and angst ridden. To this day I am incredibly grateful that my mom has such a discerning and compassionate ear.

Tricia, president of Management Research Group (MRG), and I met in person at my Midtown New York office tower high above the World's Most Famous Arena. I was struck by her Bohemian flair and cadence, but once the pleasantries, introductions, and "I just love your mother" small talk was complete, she came out swinging. I had the immediate sense that she was looking right through me with a gaze and an accompanying line of questioning that made it clear that she had "seen this act before." She peppered me with questions, trying to pry into inner thoughts that I was not ready to reveal to her or myself. Not yet, anyway. It felt as if every story I told, meeting I discussed, frustration I had, or success I mentioned was met with a similar "meh" response followed by a series of queries dismissing the "what" and trying to get at the "why." For example, beaming with pride, I described a particular deal we had just closed, the largest sponsorship deal ever in sports.

"Okay, great. Congrats. You are a conquering hero," she said. "Is there more to life than that? Is there more to you than that?" Tricia's smooth and easy style seemed to quickly vanish as a sharp, smart, and driven coach emerged, challenging me to identify who I wanted to become and why.

Tricia quickly became a confidante, friend, and guide for me. In a breakthrough meeting, she told me that, to find my inner peace, it was time to move from the warrior phase to the sage phase, another way of saying that it was time for me to become a leader whose victories are about helping others achieve their dreams and do great things. "But I love the warrior phase," I would repeatedly say back to her. She wanted me to "fight, kill, win" less and "embrace, love, teach" more.

"You can do more," she would say. "You can be more." Although I resisted, the seed had been planted. Tricia pushed me to incorporate mindfulness meditation into my life as a path to slow down and connect with myself. Nowadays, everyone is doing some form of meditation, but back then it sounded too . . . out there. Still, I tried it. Around the same time, I was in a taxi with a friend, Josh Sapan, CEO of AMC Networks, and he leaned over and said, "Do you mind if I meditate on this ride?" I encouraged him to do so, but laughed to myself at the thought of finding peace and stillness amid the hustle and bustle of New York City, the honking horns, the smells from the street, and the taxicab's sudden stops and starts. Yet he did it, and even though his head kept knocking against the window with each pothole we drove over, he remained in his meditative state. This made me think I could give meditation a try. I felt a bit silly at first, so I started focusing on my breathing in bed before I went to sleep and again when I woke up in the morning. As thoughts would come racing into my head, I would just notice that they were there and go back to my breathing. The first couple dozen times, I lasted a minute or two, but after a while I became more equipped and more effective. Finding stillness in the world in which we live has brought me clarity and even some sanity, as I am able to block out the noise and "just be."

I still smile when I think of how closed off I was to something that has ended up helping me so much. It is just a step in the journey, as I am still getting more comfortable in what Tricia calls the sage phase. Maybe you've thought about meditation. Well, it's time to give it a try. It will help you in *every* realm of your life.

At Harris Blitzer Sports & Entertainment (HBSE), a sports and entertainment holding company that includes the Philadelphia 76ers and New Jersey Devils, we've taken a number of steps to encourage people to slow down, center themselves, and connect with each other. We encourage mindfulness and meditation. In fact, we don't just *encourage* it, we help to make it happen. We have a policy that has proven more popular than I would have thought possible: you can bring your phone to the meeting, but you need to put it on a phone table out of arm's length. This has been transformative. Part of the magic of a meeting, and many of life's other experiences, is the human connection. (Just think about how disconnected so many of us felt during the Zoom meetings we attended during COVID-19.) It means that you walk into the room and *are* where your feet are. Instead of looking down, we engage in the kind of conversations that make people feel connected at a level beyond work colleagues. It starts with the kind of eye-to-eye contact and simple conversation that used to be normal: "How was the weekend? How was your daughter's soccer game? Is there anything I can do to help you?" It's not that complicated, but it matters more now than ever. Be connected, be present. Be with me. Look me in the eye and talk to me. Understand who I am as a person. Respect your neighbor.

Imagine that! All the basic stuff you learned as a child can improve your work life dramatically. That text can wait.

At HBSE, we push for mindfulness outside of the office too. For three days each summer, we curate, deliver, and host a "Go Forward" (because we do not "retreat"), our executive leadership off-site. These meetings are not about hitting aggressive revenue growth targets. We don't listen to a budget review over lunch or next year's business plan over dinner. Go Forward is about developing our employees' minds, bodies, and souls because we know it can and will help them become better leaders, executives, colleagues, parents, and friends. They will be more present in their homes, at their jobs, and in their faith.

A few years ago, our Go Forward was held at a resort tucked deep into the Pocono Mountains of Pennsylvania. Some of the exercises were led by Dr. Christine Moriconi, co-director of the Center for Contemplative

Studies at West Chester University. We were guided to her by Pat Croce, former owner of the Philadelphia 76ers, now a guru and a good friend. On that June day, Christine stood before 150 senior leaders in a ballroom lined with floor-to-ceiling windows that gave a clear and serene view of lush tree-covered mountains and a deep blue sky without a cloud in sight. "There is untapped wisdom and creativity in each of us. The key to unlocking it is stillness," Christine said.

"Mindfulness is bringing up the potential in all of us with ease," continued her co-director, Don McCown. "It's the mind breathing and stretching." For the next 15 minutes, under the soothing, methodic voices of these two industry-leading experts, the most talented, high-velocity executives in the world of sports and entertainment sat in complete, contemplative silence. It was calm and peaceful, and I could barely make out the faint sound of air conditioning blowing into the drapes.

I peeked. I'll admit it.

I peeked for a moment and it was worth it to see the fierce negotiators, hard chargers, cell junkies, sales bulldogs, and 1:00 a.m. emailers all completely still, eyes closed, shoes off on yoga mats, some sitting, some lying on their backs. A group breathing, still, and quiet . . . completely vulnerable and committed to the exercise, the time together, and being where their feet are.

Sessions like this teach us that our minds are a collection of what we think and how we live, and they encourage us to exist in the present. After all, how can I meaningfully connect with you, my colleague, my manager, my daughter, my wife, or my brother if my mind is constantly racing and unfocused? How can I be present in this meeting and respect your time and presentation efforts if I'm distracted by the noise inside my head?

★ Grounding Principle ★

I'm not saying it's easy to be completely still. But I *am* saying that it's worth it. Our ability to have more meaning is right here in front of us, but so are the distractions, and too often the distractions rule the day. *Find your peace. Find your quiet time. Find yourself.* We have to plan it, schedule it, have the discipline to stick to it, but it is a choice—our choice—and I hope you continue to make the right one, especially when things go south . . . and things always go south eventually.

Live Your Leadership Constitution

One snowy January evening in Newark, New Jersey, I was excited to be meeting a good friend, Brian Blair, who had driven down from New Canaan, Connecticut, with a buddy to join me for a New Jersey Devils hockey game. Brian's friend, Shawn Nelson, founder and CEO of Lovesac, made an instant and lasting impression on me (and not just because I always loved sitting on a Lovesac). He was interesting, but more importantly, he was interested. He connected with people and he asked a lot of questions. He was confident, but walked with an air of humility. He was funny, but not in a way that constantly made him the center of attention.

Watching sports is a great way to connect with people—you have three hours to sit next to one another. At the Devils game, we talked about our lives: our routines, family, and marriage all set against the backdrop of a swirling, intense, and sometimes chaotic life around us. We got pretty deep on a variety of topics, more quickly than usual in conversations I have with people I've just met. Shawn and I talked about times of struggle and sacrifice, times when the wind was gusting into our faces instead of at our backs, and we did so with an air of vulnerability that is unusual for top business executives in a first meeting. Shawn told me about his family values, which his wife and children say together each evening, and the mantra he repeats first thing every morning. I was intrigued, and after thinking about it for a while, I texted him later that night before I went to bed. I asked if he would share his values and mantra and he agreed:

Nelson Family Values

CLEAN thoughts, words, bodies
SMART church, books, decisions

POSITIVE attitude, actions, influence
RESPECTFUL family, elders, peers
LOVING children of God
. . . And TOUGH

These values are powerful and impactful because they provide examples and a guidepost for his family. And I believe he is on to something worth considering if you are defining what matters in your life, family, and home. We have O'Neil Family Rules too, although they're simply written on a blackboard in our kitchen and would likely have a bigger impact if we read them each night as a family. They are:

Root for each other
Respect and grace
Do not be outworked

Shawn's Morning Mantra

Shawn gets up every day and looks in the mirror and says, "This is the kind of person I want to be." More specifically, he says,

I am Heavenly Father's son and priesthood leader. I am not just faithful but valiant. I will shine today. I am excited to be with my kids every moment I can, and look for opportunities to mentor and teach them, and to be helpful to my wife. I never dodge. When I don't feel

tip-top, then I ponder this mantra or work out without hesitation. I don't drink, or gamble, or swear, or look at women. I don't have a middle-aged gut because I don't eat very much. I exhibit self-control. I will not just be pleasantly remembered but I positively impact everyone I can. I make people feel great about themselves. I deprecate myself. I seek to do service. I exude love and enthusiasm to all. I smile a lot.

Look, this may be a lot to aspire to, and we all aspire to different things, but what I love about Shawn's mantra is that it touches on faith, family, fitness, and love of others as his core direction. This is equally powerful and instructive, but more importantly it helps him try to keep his feet firmly planted on the ground and his heart, mind, and soul in the same place. What would your mantra look like? It may not look anything like Shawn's. The important part is to set an intention for your day and for your life. A daily mantra is one way to do that; another is creating a Leadership Constitution.

Create and Commit to a Leadership Constitution

My brother Michael is CEO and founder of an interactive patient care company called GetWellNetwork. Michael was diagnosed with non-Hodgkin's lymphoma while in graduate school at Georgetown. Because of his awful patient experience, he pledged to himself and anyone within earshot that if he lived through that hell, he would flip healthcare on its head. And he did. (I'll share more of Michael's story in chapter 5.)

Several years ago, I was in DC for a game and went to visit Michael at work. I was pacing around his office, waiting for him to surface from a meeting, when I was drawn to a framed and prominently placed declaration of sorts hanging right over his desk.

I DECLARE THAT I AM passionate, creative, positive, and influential. I am a change agent and a leader. I am open and honest. I value integrity and family above everything. I am competitive and ambitious, and I am energized by people coming together to win. I am a survivor. Lastly, I am humbled and grateful for life's blessing each day, yet bold in my ability and responsibility to make the world better.

YOU CAN COUNT ON ME TO bring bold, new ideas that move people and industries forward even in the face of great challenge and resistance. I will always tell the truth, even when the message is difficult to deliver, or to hear. You can count on me to be a team player, as well as an effective coach, and include others in key decisions. I will make the tough call when necessary, and bring endless energy, creativity, and focus when the stakes are the highest.

This document and its language is Michael to a T. But where did it come from, and what the heck was it doing hanging in his office? Turns out, Michael had been working with Chicago-based executive coach Rich Hill of Gabriel Consulting. He raved about the impact Rich had had on his own senior leadership team and strongly encouraged me to work with him to help shape the team at HBSE. I followed up within hours, and Rich agreed to talk a few days later. He insisted our first meeting be a video conference call. (This was long before COVID, when video calls weren't as common.) I had no trouble with that, as I use the same tactic with someone I don't know to make sure the person I am speaking with is focused, prepared, and present, not using the call as time to catch up on unread emails. But things went downhill fast.

It was just one of those days, and I was scrambling. I was in back-to-back meetings, walking quickly from the conference room to my office to the conference room again, answering emails and texts on the fly as my assistant, Denise, desperately tried to keep me close to schedule. I rushed back to my office, popped into my chair, and dialed Rich's Skype number five minutes later than our scheduled time. Apparently, this was not the best way to start off my relationship with him. "Is this call important to you?" was the first thing Rich asked. Without waiting for my answer, he went on.

"I'm busy and I'm sure you are too, but you should either commit to the call or not," he said. "I'm committed. Are you?" I was, and trust me, I was not late for one of our scheduled meetings again. Happily, tensions quickly eased, and after several sessions, Rich suggested that I, and eventually my leadership team, write our own commitment statements. All we had to do was complete the same two statements Michael had hanging in his office in his declaration: *I declare that I am* . . . and *You can count on me to* . . .

Simple? Sure. But far from easy. Do it right, and you will find yourself digging deep inside.

Rich helped me contemplate, create, and commit to a Leadership Constitution through the following guidance and focus:

- A constitution is an articulation of the core qualities that you *are*. It's not the roles you play. It's what you bring to the roles you play.
- A constitution is always expressed in the positive. There are no negative traits in a Leadership Constitution. If negative traits have found their way into your constitution, it's a function of allowing the intellect to hijack the process. Don't let it do that.

- A constitution is *not* aspirational. It's not what you want or hope or strive to be "one day." It's who you are *committed* to being. In every moment. There are *no* qualifiers, mollifiers, softeners of any kind in a constitution. None.

- A constitution is *not* based on sentiment, past behavior, or even current behavior. Often, we have core attributes that we are not living true to. When this occurs, we experience suffering—or cause suffering for those around us. Consider that there are two valid ways to arrive at core attributes: the contemplative way—simply looking deep within and noticing—*and* through observing any area in which you experience suffering. Where we suffer can nearly always be traced back to a core attribute that our actions and behavior are not lining up with.

- A constitution is what you stand for. It's the qualities that you *are*, that matter most to you, because you say so. It's not merely what you think of yourself, and it has nothing to do with opinions you may have of yourself or judgments you may hold against yourself. It's a bold, audacious statement of your core.

- A constitution, once articulated, is *practiced* through the act of declaring with witnesses who will hold you accountable.

Rich provided incredible feedback along the way and challenged each sentence. He pushed me to resist the temptation to complete it in a day or even a week, but instead to pressure test it with people I love and who know me the best. Rich urged me to read it out loud with conviction in front of the mirror, much like Shawn does each morning, to see where it was strong and where it felt stretched. While my Leadership Constitution is below, it is only here so that you can start to think about creating one for yourself.

I declare that I am a passionate and authentic leader of leaders who feels a gravitational pull toward talent and character. I wear my heart on my sleeve. I love people and being part of a team. I get energy from helping others and would give the shirt off my back to a stranger and anything, anytime to a friend. I am a family-first, high-integrity, and surprisingly sensitive change agent who is confident, caring, and intellectually curious. This fuels a competitive drive that at times feels like a chip on my shoulder.

You can count on me to . . .

- bring positive energy into my space
- exude urgency and push you, challenge you, nudge you, and raise the bar beyond your ex-

pectations and sometimes what you think reasonable

- laugh with you, cry with you, love you, even when you won't laugh, haven't cried, and don't feel loved
- root for you today, every day, and always
- share the most personal of thoughts, emotions, stories, highs, and lows, because I am okay with it and who I am
- enjoy the roller-coaster of life, whether we are going forward, backward, or upside down
- drive hard to reach the summit and then quickly start on another mountain
- share wins and take hits for losses

★ Grounding Principle ★

Committing in writing to life and a way of living matters. Whether we have family rules or values, whether we have a morning mantra or a Leadership Constitution, we need guideposts in our lives. We need reinforcement in terms of what we stand for, what matters, and what we prioritize, and through those things we can be where our feet are when it counts. *Life is better, more fulfilling, and more rewarding when you are where your feet are, and the good news is that it is up to you to decide and commit,* as the formula is very simple. That does not mean it is easy, but I *can* say that it is worth the effort.

✒ Your Turn to Put This into Practice ✒

There are times when you can passively read a book and other times when you actively engage. My promise to you is that when you actively engage in the exercises at the end of each chapter in this book, you will learn more, retain more, and move a step closer toward the person you aspire to be. It is time for you to write your Leadership Constitution, by completing the following:

I declare that I am . . .
You can count on me to . . .

You take it from here. The first draft will not be your final draft, and that's okay. Practice by speaking in front of the mirror and to someone who loves you and knows you best. After feedback, take another shot to refine and then finalize your version.

CHAPTER 2

Change the Race

Everybody has a plan until you get
punched in the face.
—Mike Tyson

Unfortunately, bad things happen to good people, oftentimes when least expected. For the most part, difficult times make us stronger and, with the right perspective, help us learn and grow. Sometimes, however, it gets so rough that we find ourselves trapped in despair, uncertain about how to get out of the funk we are in. I once found myself sinking into almost unbearable sadness. Walking through that fire helped me learn and identify a process to better cope the next time I fall. It's called changing the race. Changing the race can be useful in any situation of difficulty, loss, or sadness. It has three essential components: (1) recognize that you can choose to change your situation; (2) run toward the storm instead of away from it, acknowledge your pain rather than deny it; (3) find your center with the help of people you care about and who care about you.

Recognize You Have a Choice
Strength, Friendship, and Loss

My time in the barrel—one of them—came at a point when everything was going well. It was one of those streaks when every part of life—health, relationships, work, strength of faith, school, learning, and friendships—was in sync. My career as the CEO of the Philadelphia 76ers and New Jersey Devils was fulfilling, and our teams were beginning to show tremendous promise, my 20-plus-year marriage was full of support, fun, and love, my daughters were in a groove with friends, school, each other, and our family, and my strengthening faith enveloped me. Of course, things were not perfect—life is always a roller-coaster, and this one had fewer loops and twists—but I had finally discovered the ability to be where my feet are, and I was squarely focused on my WMI (what's most important). But as John Lennon sang, "Life is what happens to you when you're busy making other plans."

So life happened, and all of a sudden the sync was gone and the roller-coaster was stopped midride, suspended upside down on its biggest loop.

Wil Cardon and I met at Harvard Business School,

and he had become much more than a friend—he was like a brother. He was Uncle Wil in our house, and I was Uncle Blue in his. (Why "Blue"? I broke my leg when I was five years old, and when my cast was removed months later there were blue spots on my leg. They turned out to be remnants of candy that had slipped into my cast. My brothers found this hysterical and never let me forget it. Wil picked up on this nickname after spending time with us.) Wil was a force of nature who loved to laugh and make others laugh, and he had a mischievous and playful manner that brought light to every dark room.

When Wil was determined to do something, there was no way to stop him, and oh by the way, you were coming with him. Midnight ice cream run? No. Wil, it's too late, I'm tired, I have to walk the dog . . . then I would find myself in the car with the others he had coaxed along for the ride and the laughs, watching wide-eyed as he devoured four massive scoops of ice cream.

Costco run while in Cabo, Mexico? No. Wil, I just want to hit the beach, can we just chill? Amazingly, 30 minutes later, I would find myself buying the largest licorice barrel on the planet.

Triple cheeseburger with Animal Style fries at In-N-Out? No. Wil, it's midnight, I am trying to cut back, and fast food, really? Predictably and shortly thereafter,

I would be sitting under neon lights eating a very large burger ordered off a secret menu then heading to his house after he had canceled my hotel reservation.

When Wil was at his best, he gave all he had in time, love, and attention to his friends and family. But there was another side to him. Wil suffered from crippling depression. If you were close to him, you could tell when he was in that dark place: he wouldn't return texts or phone calls, his voicemail would fill up, and he was unable to get out of bed. He'd checked into facilities a few times, where the doctors would try different combinations of medication to get him back on his feet. During Wil's darkest moments, my role, as I saw it, was to love him, talk to him, wake him, and remind him how amazing he was.

One hot August evening I was brushing my teeth getting ready for bed when I got a call from our mutual friend Jared Stone.

"Hey," I answered, momentarily thinking it was an odd time for him to call.

"I have some bad news," he said, his voice missing its usual energy.

"Are you okay?" I asked.

"It's not me. It's Wil. He's no longer with us."

Jared went on to tell me that Wil had taken his own life while staying at his summer cabin in Flagstaff, Arizona. I didn't hear anything after that. I'm not even sure I hung up the phone. Typically an emotional over-crier, I was devoid of feeling as I walked downstairs to our family room, where I told Lisa the news, directly and catatonically.

"We have to tell the girls before they see something on social media or get a text," she said. Lisa's eyes welled with tears as she reached for my hand. I remained numb, totally numb. I stared straight ahead and robotically walked into the kitchen, where Alexa, Kira, and Eliza were huddled over the family computer, laughing loudly as they watched old videos of themselves.

I launched in. "I just wanted to tell you that Uncle Wil is dead. Uh, I mean, he is no longer with us. Well, he killed himself, shot himself actually. It was suicide."

It sounds harsh because it *was* harsh. Usually in a situation like this, I try to console my kids. I am quick with a hug and an "I love you." Any dad skills I had at that moment, though, went out the window

I glanced at Lisa, and her look said it all: not exactly something for the "Dad of the Year" folder. She picked up the pieces with the girls. As I walked up the staircase to our bedroom, the downward spiral began . . . I was in pieces, and they were spread too far out to be picked up by anybody, even Lisa.

I had been with Wil two weeks earlier for a long weekend in Myrtle Beach, South Carolina, for O'Bats—a baseball tournament that my three brothers and I put on every year that hosts 50 friends from our childhood, school, work, and every part of life in between. We get together to laugh, love, and have some reprieve from the grind of life. It is pure unadulterated fun. We draft teams and compete in a bracket-style tournament. We have uniforms, sing "The Star-Spangled Banner," have a public address announcer, and even hold a post-tournament award ceremony. It was clear throughout the weekend that Wil was struggling, but I didn't really get it. I mean, I *knew* he was suffering from depression, I just didn't *get* it. "Choose to make good choices. Choose to smile. Choose to have fun. Maybe you should exercise, eat better, sleep more. Do some service for others," I told him. "That's what I do when I'm down."

Like I said, I didn't get it. Ugh, what was I thinking and why couldn't I have done something?

The day after Wil died, I called his wife, Nicole. I mumbled some unintelligible words: I love you, I miss him, I am so sorry, I will pray for you and the kids, blah blah blah. (Think Charlie Brown teacher–like sound.) I was lost and at a loss for words. I wanted to say that everything would be okay, but I couldn't see a path for myself and couldn't bear to consider the road ahead for the Cardon family. Then Nicole stopped me, my wondering, and my lost mind and asked if I would speak at the funeral the following week.

I didn't know what to say.

"Really? Okay, maybe, I mean, yes, really? Uh, of course, of course, I am honored," I finally replied, already feeling the fog thickening around me. (Years later, I am actually crying uncontrollably on the plane as I reconstruct this moment. Ever sit next to that guy crying on the plane? Pretty awesome treat.)

"There is only one person Wil would want speaking: you," Nicole said. I hung up quickly so she wouldn't hear me burst into tears. That night I started thinking and writing, speaking mostly to Wil's five kids. *How am I going to do this in a way that says what they need to hear?* I was trying to make it a celebration of the good parts of Wil's life while ignoring the depression, but still wanting them to know that it wasn't okay to take your own life, ever. My emotions were flying in every direction: some sad, some mad, some happy, some relieved, and some aching. I would settle down just long enough to be jolted by a moment or memory or trip or thing Wil said or did that flooded my brain and then my heart. The spiraling would continue. I cried more in the week between Jared's call and the funeral than I had in the previous ten years of my life combined.

Lisa, Alexa, Kira, Eliza, and I flew to Arizona for the funeral. The weather was classic Arizona summer: scorching, cook-an-egg-on-the-ground hot. The night before the funeral, we went to a reception at the hotel with friends who had flown in from around the world. Everybody had a Wil story or two to share, and we took turns telling them until the wee hours of the morning. This was clearly what I needed. The day of the funeral I woke up early and refreshed for the first time since Jared's call. I was ready, even smiling a bit. I quietly left our casita and worked out in the resort gym and then went on a walk—check. Went back to our little hotel bungalow and talked to my kids about Wil's suicide and reminded them how important it was to get help when you needed it—check. I told them I loved them. "Dad, we know. Dad, we love you. Dad, you will be great. Dad, Uncle Wil will be happy you are doing this." Uh oh, I started to cry again.

I pulled it together and left ahead of them to go to the church. I put on some awful country music, thinking Wil might be here with me and he would get a kick out of the music and my distaste for it. I arrived in the parking lot and sat in the car for a minute. *I'm okay. I've got this*, I thought. Shifting back into my Type A, live-event-manager mode, I made my way inside to figure out the logistics and ran into Bishop Ord, who was there to conduct the service. Lisa and I had met him the night before while setting up chairs with him, his wife, and a lot of friends.

"How are you doing?" he asked. Before I could say, "Awesome. Great. Feeling good," I lost it again. *Oh boy*.

Wil and I belonged to the same faith, the Church of Jesus Christ of Latter-day Saints, which is organized around 12 apostles like the original Christian Church. The apostles are our spiritual leaders. I had heard that two of them, Elder Andersen and Elder Ballard, both close friends of Wil and his family, were attending, but I didn't realize they were both speaking until I looked at the program. Wait, what? *At least I don't have to go before the two of them*, I thought. But then I glanced at the program again. *Oh wait, yes I do. I'm up first!* At that moment, the cool air conditioning in the church was no match for the heat flash of nerves that rushed up my body to my neck and then my head as a small bead of sweat dropped from my brow onto my notes. To say I felt inadequate, overwhelmed, and ill-equipped would be an understatement.

The funeral was held at the Arcadia Stake Center—a huge church building filled wall to wall with seating for about a thousand. Yet, even with its immense size, it was standing room only, with additional people sandwiched in nearby classrooms typically used for Sunday school classes, each equipped with TVs to broadcast the service. It wasn't the crowd that I found daunting or the public speaking. (Give me any topic and a few bullet points and I am one of the rare people who actually enjoy it.) It was the fact that I was speaking at my best friend's funeral—that's a job that no one wants. I knew I had one chance to celebrate this amazing guy's life with his wife and kids in the front row staring up at me, and yet I couldn't think straight.

I settled into a chair on the stand in front of the church as people continued to file in. Beautiful organ music started, and as I was reviewing my notes, a strong hand landed on my arm, squeezing it like a vise, jolting me out of my fog and back to where my feet were. I looked up. *Gulp.* It was Elder Andersen.

"Brother O'Neil, why are you sitting all the way over here?" he asked, referring to the seat I'd chosen, the farthest away from everyone else to the right on the stage.

"Um, well, uh, I was thinking I should stay out of the way . . ." My voice trailed off.

"No. That will not do. Come with me," he said. As we moved across the stage, all the eyes in the church seemed to be following our every step, not looking at me, of course, but fixated on one of the two beloved apostles in attendance as he guided me to a seat right next to him. I was a bit intimidated . . . okay, maybe a lot intimidated, but it was a welcome reset and distraction.

After the service opened with one of the longest prayers in the pantheon of long prayers, I felt that same viselike grip on my arm, this time knowing it was Elder Andersen. Hoping he might loosen it a bit and wondering if he had been spending some extra time in the weight room, I heard a not-so-subtle and very stern directive whispered in my ear. "This is not entertainment. This is a holy service," he said. *What was he referring to?* I wondered. I had zoned out completely and had not heard much of the prayer. I took out a pen and crossed out the jokes I'd planned to open with, and as I was trying to figure out how to begin, I was introduced and called to the stand. I slowly walked to the front and looked out over a full, reverent, and loving group. Then I saw the Cardon family and my eyes didn't leave them for the rest of the talk.

I cried a few times. I was tapped on the shoulder a few times to wrap it up as I went a little longer than expected. (I smiled and almost laughed out loud because Wil would have loved me shaking off the brass and finishing my talk.) I could feel the spirit so strongly in the church that my chest pounded as if it were coming through my shirt. And, just like that, it was over. As I sat down, Elder Andersen leaned in close to me, this time without the grip.

"Wil's children will never forget that talk, Brother O'Neil. Well done," he said. My sense of grief was temporarily replaced by relief and then an awkward sense of pride that felt out of place, and then quickly relief again that it was over. I put my hands over my face and sobbed as quietly as I could through the rest of the service.

I'd like to say that speaking at the funeral helped me move forward, but in truth the fog would return. The weeks and months that followed were a really heavy period in my life. I generally wake up happy, but that was not the case during this time. Whatever depression is, I think I had some version of it—or maybe it was experiencing grief for the first time. I was in the type of fog where someone would call my name three times and I wouldn't look up. The type of fog where I was just staring into space like New York City subway commuters who need to get off that treadmill. There was still no life in my eyes. If I was in a meeting and something reminded me of Wil, I had to get up and walk out, head straight to my office, and cry. I had encountered more than a few tough times and tragedies before, but this felt different. I prayed, read, and meditated, but I could not shake myself from the gloom that engulfed me.

★ Grounding Principle ★

I had to change the race to break out of the funk I was in, and with time and some encouragement, I began to open up to family, friends, and colleagues. I began seeking thoughts, stories, and prayers from my community and actively listening to similar stories of pain. People I'd known only as strong and confident confessed intimate moments of vulnerability and sadness. Each story was unique, but there were consistent themes: *Isolation is today's kryptonite. The path toward overcoming our most difficult times is through opening ourselves up, seeking help, listening, and engaging those we love.*

The more people I connected with, the more clearly I began to see the world. I could breathe again. I could laugh again. It wasn't like a light switch, of course; more like a dimmer that slowly provided more and more light.

Run Toward the Storm

The first thing you notice when you meet Lara Toscani Weems (or LTW to those of us fortunate enough to work with her) is her pace—she is always moving a hundred miles per hour. You learn very quickly that she's a smart, driven, and hard-charging powerhouse who works in a higher gear than most of the world. What you don't see is the incredible pain, suffering, anger, mourning, and fighting for life that she's endured. When I hired her, I knew that her son, Carter, had been born with special needs, but I had *no* idea about the story of how she got to be where she was . . . or how close to the cliff it was until three years later, when she opened our company's annual Go Forward event with Carter's story and her journey.

The way Lara tells it, life was golden for the first couple decades of her life: she grew up in the "right" zip code with a supportive family, scored a Division 1 track-and-field scholarship to William & Mary, and even received a fellowship to graduate school. At the age of 25, she became the youngest marketing director in a major sports and entertainment corporation and had a near perfect wedding at a five-star hotel to a handsome college football player turned attorney. Aaron was the steady and stable counterpoint to Lara's frenetic pace and energy, and the two were a perfect match. Soon after, a new house, and the clockwork pregnancy at the age of 28. Nine months later, she had that golden moment holding her newborn son, Carter, thinking, *NOW I have everything. Everything that really matters.* That moment lasted just 24 hours.

Carter was born with a rare liver defect that caused the toxin ammonia to seep from his liver into the rest of his body, poisoning his organs, muscles, and brain. The formal diagnosis was ornithine transcarbamylase deficiency, but the doctors compared it to a leaky faucet. "Ammonia will drip into his brain each day until he receives a liver transplant. But he must be 20 pounds before we will put him on the transplant list, so we need to keep him alive until then," they told Lara. It could take nine months to a year for Carter to get to 20 pounds, which seemed to be an eternity. Although there was medication that could attempt to keep the levels down, it was unproven, and it couldn't stop the toxin from poisoning his little body every minute of every day.

"This will cause permanent brain damage," the doctor added. Lara ran to find a trash can so she could vomit, barely making it.

"What happens to the brain with damage like this?" Lara asked.

"We don't know. At minimum, developmental delays could be expected."

"Will he walk and talk?"

"Maybe, maybe not," the doctor said.

"Throw a baseball? Swing on swings?"

"We don't know. Maybe, maybe not."

"Breathe on his own or swallow food?"

"We don't know. Maybe, maybe not."

"What about hug me? Will he know I'm his mom?" Lara asked.

"We don't know . . ."

The uncertainty was awful and, as Lara describes it, a plunge into darkness. For weeks and weeks, Lara and Aaron lived 24/7 in the neonatal intensive care unit (NICU), then the pediatric intensive care unit (PICU), where Carter lay on a metal platform under heat lamps all day, unconscious, hovering between life and death.

"It was emotionally, physically, and spiritually unbearable, even for the doctors and nurses who I'd catch crying or burying their faces in their hands," Lara says. Twice-daily blood tests indicated Carter's progress, if any. An ammonia level reading of 75 was a victorious day; 200 was concerning; 400 was a "let's take some pictures holding him tonight, because he most likely won't wake up tomorrow" type day. Unfortunately, they experienced several of those days.

Three weeks after Carter was born, the doctors ushered Lara and Aaron into a small conference room where the results of Carter's CAT scan were projected on the wall. The shape of a human brain was unmistakable; it was bright white against a gray background. About 20–25 percent of the white brain was shaded with defined, but scattered, patches of black. As the doctor began to summarize the findings, Lara interrupted him.

"It's the black parts, right? The black, clouded parts are the inflamed and poisoned and damaged parts of the brain?" she said, sure of her analysis.

"The poisoned portions, Mrs. Weems," the doctor began, "are white . . ."

As Lara tells it, she became a shadow. Not a mother, not a nurse, not the person she'd been before. "I was a rising star and young executive who left my career completely to care for my dying child. I was an outgoing young woman with a passion for people, adventure, and activity—who, by necessity, became a germaphobe full of emotional distress and cut off every person in my life aside from a few family members. The pillars of my personality and self-confidence were shattered. I summarized my life as: No running (my escape). No job (my identity). No friends (my connection)." This is a dark place that I hope you have never been and never have to visit.

As they waited for Carter to gain enough weight to be eligible for the transplant list, Lara and Aaron brought him home, not the joyous homecoming most people experience with a newborn, but one with so many rules: if Carter threw up his medication, he would get more brain damage; if he caught a cold, he would get more brain damage; if he cut a tooth and had a fever, he would get more brain damage. Too much medication, too little medication, the wrong amount of protein powder—the result of almost any ill footing was "more brain damage." The pressure was insurmountable, the sorrow incalculable, and the grief all-encompassing.

Lara was lost and without hope.

"Every day I was watching my son die. Every day I was holding him knowing there was poison seeping into his brain, and no one could stop it. Drip. Drip. Drip," Lara explains. "Every day I knew he'd be able to do less than the day before. Every day we wondered, is he sleeping soundly? Or lapsing into a coma? Every day I pretended the world outside my home didn't exist. It simply hurt too much to think of it moving forward happily—without me. And I would never be part of that world again." Even more painful was seeing posts of her friends' children on social media, their lives advancing in real time, celebrating together at birthday parties and football games—events to which she was not invited.

After nine dark months, Carter was placed in a priority position on the liver transplant list. Finally, on a sunny day in May, a nurse took Carter from Lara and wheeled him into surgery. Then Lara walked into the waiting room, lay down on the cold, bare floor, and immediately fell asleep. "For the first time in nine months I slept without fear or worry. Carter's life was in someone else's hands," she says. "I awoke to find a nurse had draped a thin sheet over me, and the doctor reporting that surgery had gone perfectly and the liver fit like it was meant to be Carter's."

This was the first step in Lara's long journey in finding herself again. Slowly Lara allowed select aunts, old teammates, and girlfriends to visit. Once Lara realized she could attach Carter's medication and food pump to her not-yet-used jogging stroller and walk down a trail by the river, she decided she would walk him for each nap. "I would jog for a few seconds, then peek inside the stroller to see if the pump was still intact. My heart was beating faster for the first time in a year and there was a trail and a river and sunshine." Running is Lara's escape—it fuels and resets her psyche. And it was beginning to make a difference.

There wasn't one big magical moment that brought Lara back, but hundreds of small ones. Hundreds of runs. Hundreds of deep conversations with an aunt, a loving parent, or her sister. Little moments of joy—like seeing a tulip creep up through the snow. Little victories. Little hints of normalcy. But she was still isolating herself—she needed human connection.

Slowly, Lara let in those people she trusted, including a mentor and former boss she'd known since she was 20 years old. With tears welling in her eyes, she approached him and said, "I think I need to work again. Do you have *anything* for me?" He was quiet, brows furrowed. "I can't imagine a more unattractive job candidate than the woman with the chronically ill child who just has copped to seeing a therapist," Lara says. "But he called a week later with a job with the Harlem Globetrotters. I fumbled like a baby elephant on ice skates, shocked how quickly I'd forgotten almost everything I'd known in my past work life. Things hadn't turned out how I'd planned them, but I was making progress." She needed to be around other people and to feel herself accomplishing, achieving, and focusing her incredible energy.

Other friends came through simply by listening. One day, she opened up about her fears for the future to her friend Leslie. "What will I do when Carter is 25 years old, and we're living in a house of wheelchairs, ramps, and pulleys from ceilings? What will he *do* every day when he's 25? What happens when he's 40 and he's far too big for me to carry? Where will we live? What if the liver fails in a few years?" Lara asked her friend.

"But you don't know those fears will come true, do you?"

"No," Lara replied, convincing herself that she needed to start living more and worrying less.

The day Carter was fitted for his first wheelchair, three therapists raced circles around him adjusting harnesses, straps, and buckles to his exact height and positioning needs while he arched and screamed. Then after a moment, he settled. It was, perhaps, the first time in his life he was supported the way his little body, muscles, and limbs needed. He calmed and relaxed. "One half of my heart wanted to cry tears of joy to see my son supported properly and sitting quietly, observing the world around him without pain. But now there was no faking it. He was not just a little boy who 'looked tired' in an umbrella stroller, as so many strangers in the street would offer without solicitation. We now had a family member in a wheelchair. This was his *first* wheelchair, in a lifetime of wheelchairs," Lara explains. "*Better get used to this*, I thought. At the time, it was like an induction to a fraternity that I wanted nothing to do with. Fortunately now, it's one I am beamingly proud to be a part of."

Lara knows her son will never walk with his father down a trail in Yosemite National Park. He will never go to the prom. He will never stay out too late with his friends and get into harmless and memory-making trouble. He will never sleep on the top bunk at camp. Never get married. But Lara pushes through. The loss of a dream you've carried with you your entire life is very significant. "But I'm not settling for second place—I'm just running in a different race, and this is one I am winning. I've already spent too much time in the gray. I intend to spend the rest of it running, climbing mountains, chasing the extraordinary, and loving *hard*. I choose life. I choose to throw all of my emotion and soul into everything I do because it should *all* matter. It should matter because the alternative is that you have no life or hope or joy or future. I've been there, and I'm never, ever going back."

★ Grounding Principle ★

Lara has a sign hanging over the desk in her office that reads, "You can have it all." I'm in awe every time I think about her and her journey. She changed her perspective on her son's diagnosis, took in the world, took on the world, changed the race, and moved forward in life. She ran toward the storm instead of away from it. Lara recognized her darkness and began to heal when she let people back into her life and was once again fueled by the energy of her career.

We need each other more today than ever before as support systems, sounding boards, and sometimes a rescue. *This experience knocked Lara down but not out. It gave her—and everyone blessed enough to meet her—a new perspective on what it means to have it all and the confidence and commitment to change the race.*

A First (But Not Last) Public Failure

As I mentioned earlier, one of my more public failures was the rise and then crash, burn, and fall of a small and short-lived startup called HoopsTV. In comparison to Wil's death or Lara's journey, my story may seem relatively inconsequential, but your personal storm always seems a lot bigger when you're in its eye.

Two years into my job as a director of sponsorship sales with the Philadelphia Eagles, I left to get an MBA from Harvard Business School, with the promise from

Jeffrey Lurie, chairman and CEO of the club, that I would always be welcomed back. Eighteen months later, I returned and was made vice president of sales, where I worked for Joe Banner and Len Komoroski. The training that I'd just received was wholly focused on preparing me to be a CEO, so even though I was just 28 years old, I was pretty certain I was equipped to be one. In reality, of course, I was not even ready to be a vice president. While I was excited and wanted to talk strategy, budgets, and business planning and to prepare for a new stadium build, the Eagles were more interested in me selling more suites and tickets. Reflecting back, sadly, the people I worked for were more right than I was about what I knew and how much I could contribute.

Around this time, my good friend Seth Berger, founder and CEO of AND1, then the number-two basketball sneaker company in the United States, asked me if I wanted to start a business with him. We brainstormed and came up with what we thought was a billion-dollar idea. HoopsTV would turn your computer into a 24-hour basketball network. For those of you scoring at home, this was the high-flying period of the dot-com-boom days, and it actually seemed like a sound plan and decision to leave a stable environment working for people I admired to chase the big idea. We worked nights developing a business plan. I was still paying off steep graduate school loans, so I didn't have a cent to contribute, but AND1 put up the first $1 million and we raised the rest, $15 million in total, on a business plan and Seth's reputation. We put together a strong team and acquired great content.

There was just one problem: this was a video-heavy site, launching well before Wi-Fi became ubiquitous and years before you could watch video on your computer. The iPad was still ten years in the future, as were smartphones. In hindsight, nobody being able to actually see the best content was more than just a bad break—it probably should have been foreseen by the president of the company (me). Looking back, I might rephrase the approach from "the best content wins" to "the best content that people can actually *watch* has a chance to win."

When I think of this experience, it reminds me of the story about the two shoe salesmen who went off to a foreign land where nobody was wearing shoes.

"No market here, nobody wears shoes," one salesman reported back.

"This is a goldmine of opportunity," said the other salesman. "Everybody here needs shoes."

In the story of HoopsTV, I was the second guy. Still, the issue was more than just the strategy being too far ahead of its time. I had this vision of what a president was and "should" do, and my list had 30 items on it instead of three main priorities. I should have spent all my time on fundraising, adjusting content to fit the current technological reality, and driving revenue. Had my focus been on those three things, the business might have had a fighting chance. Ultimately, we could not raise money at a price worthy of keeping the business going. In other words, we might have been able to raise money, but if we did, it would have wiped out all the previous investors because the price we could raise at was too low and the amount of money we needed was too high. And then in the blink of an eye, it was over. We had been jet-setting around the country meeting with Phil Knight of Nike and NBA commissioner David Stern; now we were reducing our business to fit in a filing cabinet. I was the last remaining employee and spent the final couple months negotiating out of agreements and shutting it all down. I apologized to our investors. I fired over 50 people, including good friends and even my brother Matt! Yes, I can say—with the same overinflated confidence I left business school with—that it was a miserable time in my life.

I was out of work, out of luck, and out of money, with Lisa at home raising our first child, 14-month-old Alexa. I wasn't really sure what to do, who to call, or where to go. On top of my loan payments for business school, the bills were piling up. A foreclosure notice (or two) came, which Lisa hid from me, along with anything else she thought might cause added stress. She would tell me about the bills and notices once I had a job. (She did what she thought best to get my head right and help me back on my feet, but it was not great digging out of that mess. We ended up using one of those debt consolidation companies you see on late-night TV called AmeriDebt, and it shredded our credit for seven years, making everything more expensive. Brutal, but lesson learned.)

Have you ever been in one of those places where you just feel stuck? That's where you could find me at the time. I slept a lot, watched movies, and ran mindless errands. I had to change the race, and fortunately for me, I married a strong, compassionate, understanding, and intuitive woman. Lisa used a delicate mix of just letting me be, loving comfort, and not-so-subtle pushes to go find some basketball pick-up games (my head-clearing escape from the world) to experience more human connection. She pushed me to read more (because learning helps shape and refocus the mind) and spend extra time with Alexa, who had just started to walk (because the love of a child is centering and healing). After a while, everything took hold, and my head was clear. I came home after a long stroll in the rain with Alexa, and as I walked through the door, I proclaimed, "Okay, I am ready to get back to work." Lisa smiled and said, "That is great! What's the plan?"

For three months, I had not picked up the phone to make a single phone call, but that day when I was ready, I started dialing, and over the next few days I made over two hundred phone calls to people I knew in and around the sports business. Within a week, I had four interviews with the premier brands in sports: the National Football League, Reebok, Anschutz Entertainment Group, and the National Basketball Association. Thanks to Seth Berger's rousing endorsement to Adam Silver, the current NBA commissioner, I was hired within a month to work for the accomplished Dr. Bernie Mullin and alongside the legendary Dr. Bill Sutton as a vice president at the NBA in a newly formed group called Team Marketing and Business Operations. This would change the trajectory of my career, my life, and my approach to both going forward.

★ Grounding Principle ★

I am different, better, and more evolved because of what I learned during my out-of-work, out-of-luck, and out-of-money period. As scary and confusing as it was, it brought me a new sense of what it meant to run a business, to find some humility, and to reset and reshape my approach to my career and life. My deep funk was lifted when I changed the race: I read, exercised, and committed to finding my authenticity. Intellectual curiosity through reading and learning brought me clarity and opened my mind. One book Lisa suggested during that period was *Leadership and Self-Deception* by the Arbinger Institute. It was so transformational in helping me clear out of that funk that everyone who has worked with me at the NBA,

Madison Square Garden, and HBSE has had to read it before they start.

A pickup hoop run is still a way for me to escape the world, and I know I need that in my life. There is something about the sound of the bouncing ball, the anxiety before we shoot for teams, and the competitive fight to hold the court that stays with me today. In fact, you can find me dribbling, passing, shooting, and talking trash before every 76ers game in our training complex in Camden, New Jersey. While you might not be much for the court, your physical health drives your well-being, whether it's through a spin class, yoga, or a long run. Last, that time with Alexa, taking long walks and runs to the grocery store together, buckling her in her car seat, making her lunch, and reading her bedtime stories, helped me better understand the foundation of love and life. The time we have with our children is precious, and being and staying connected with my three daughters is the gift that keeps on giving (except when they were teenagers—just kidding, partly kidding).

The Bottom Line

The bottom line is this: we all have times when things aren't going well—family, work, life, money. It happens. Some of these experiences are so bad that they engulf every waking moment for weeks, months, even years—a death in the family, divorce, miscarriage, cancer, depression, or a leaky liver of a newborn son. The most critical things to keep in mind include knowing when you need to change the race you are running and not shutting down—remember that isolation is your kryptonite when things are going badly. Engage people in your life and do not let ego or pride get in the way of good decision-making or getting help.

✿ Your Turn to Put This into Practice ✿

Commit to moments that matter. I received this email from Jim Leonard, a friend at work, when his father passed away:

> It is with a heavy heart that I write to tell you that my dad passed away around 7:30 p.m. this evening. I was holding his hand when he died, and his passing was very peaceful. He did the best he could to find joy in life after tragically losing his wife a year ago, but in the end it was time for them to be reunited.
>
> This past year has been an emotional nightmare, and I can't thank you enough for being there for me. I will be forever grateful for your thoughts and prayers during these past 12 months.
>
> I am so thankful that he waited for me to get here today before passing. As is usually the case with my dad, I walked into an 85-degree room and immediately chirped at him about the tropical climate. I then turned off the heat and opened the window. After Dad died, my wife (Patty O'Shaughnessy)

told me of an Irish wives' tale that says you open a
window so that a person's soul can peacefully depart. I
guess he just needed me to open the window for him.

I will share arrangements when we have them
finalized. Your continued support is truly appreciated.
Please share this news with others whom I might miss
as I try to get things in order.
Jim

Three days later, he sent a follow-up email that stopped me in my tracks:

Over the weekend I challenged my wife and daughter
to do one thing a month that Dad loved in order to
keep his legacy fresh. Some I think will be fairly easy
for them (grab a pizza, eat ice cream with chocolate
sauce, watch birds). Others will be a little more time-
consuming but will provide an opportunity to reflect
on the man and his life (go for a hike, volunteer for a
cause). And one will be an experience the three of us
will do together—visit Glacier National Park, where
Dad served for two years as a ranger naturalist (well it
was either Montana or visiting Kessler Air Force Base
in Mississippi. Guess which one my family picked?).

This is applicable today in your life but it takes planning, process, and the commitment to execute. For each month, identify and commit to a moment that matters with someone who matters. Some can be small acts, like writing a birthday card to your mother, or larger ones, like volunteering for a charity.

MONTH	THE PERSON WHO MATTERS	ACTIVITY/COMMITMENT
January		
February		
March		
April		
May		
June		
July		
August		
September		
October		
November		
December		

CHAPTER 3

WMI

The main thing is to keep the main thing
the main thing.
—Stephen Covey

When HBSE acquired the Prudential Center in Newark, New Jersey, I was excited to dive into a part of the industry that was new to me: the entertainment business beyond professional team sports. This involves booking concerts, family shows like Disney on Ice, and sporting events like college basketball, UFC, and boxing. Today, the Prudential Center is consistently ranked as a top-ten-booked building in North America by *Billboard* magazine, but shortly after HBSE acquired it, that ranking was hovering in the mid-20s. Sean Saadeh, who had previously opened the Barclays Center in Brooklyn to rave reviews, was hired to set our strategy. He is all music all the time. He even dresses the part: dark jeans, black t-shirt, and Converse kicks. One month into his tenure at HBSE, Sean set meetings for the two of us in L.A. with the industry's most influential and connected music executives. Our itinerary included powerhouse CEOs like Michael Rapino of Live Nation, Irving Azoff of Azoff MSG Entertainment, Tim Leiweke of Oak View Group, and Jay Marciano of AEG Presents—who bring the world's most incredible artists to the biggest stages. There were also agents and managers from CAA, WME, and UTA. Sean then added an unfamiliar name to our schedule: Marty Erlichman.

"Who?" I asked as we were reviewing our wall-to-wall schedule on the plane.

"Marty's a major player, a friend, and music-industry icon," Sean explained. "He's been Barbra Streisand's manager for over 40 years. This meeting is important."

"Great. I can't wait."

"The thing is . . . he's probably not going to like you very much," Sean said in a not-so-optimistic tone.

"What? . . . Me? . . . C'mon? . . . Why not? . . . Really?" I replied, feeling less and less certain the longer I spoke.

"Yeah, he's not going to like this whole *thing* you've got going on," he said, gesturing at my very corporate-looking suit and tie.

"So, maybe I shouldn't meet him?"

"No, no, no, you should. But did you happen to bring a pair of jeans?"

I hadn't.

We landed and headed straight from the airport to meet Marty in the lobby of the Old Hollywood–style Beverly Hills Hotel. He was right out of Central Casting for a movie star's agent, sitting in a chunky brown leather chair with a drink already in hand. I could picture him in the exact spot 30 years earlier smoking a cigar and telling stories with the same wry smile and twinkle in his eyes. I was instantly pulled in by this force of nature. About an hour into our meeting, Marty leaned over the table. His eyes widened beneath his dark-rimmed glasses as he asked if I wanted to learn the secret to life.

"Of course," I said. *What an opportunity*, I thought as I whipped my phone out of my inside suit jacket pocket.

"What are you doing?" Marty asked.

"If you're about to tell me the secret to life, I'm going to capture it so I can go home and share it with my daughters," I said. He just laughed, but in the way that a parent might at a young child saying something foolish. Recognizing this look made me smile . . . as I hit Record.

"Are you serious with the phone?" Marty asked as the video continued rolling.

"Yes. Are *you* serious about teaching me the secret to life?" I replied.

"Yes, very serious."

"Let's go, then," I said, thinking this could be one of those life-defining lessons that the universe occasionally drops in our laps.

"Number one," he said: "Wake up in the morning, put your feet on the ground, and be so passionate about what you do for work that you sprint to the office every day." *I can live that*, I thought. *That's me.* My excitement and love of what I do is part of my WMI, which, as I've mentioned, stands for "what's most important."

"Number two: At night, after a hard-charging day of work, sprint home with equal passion." A second and even more critical part of my WMI is my family. Both secrets were simple, poignant reminders: truly focus on what's most important.

For me, as it clearly is for Marty, that includes a love of work and the passion in what we do and the joy I can find at home. Shared in this chapter are stories about those who identify, prioritize, and live their WMI to hopefully help you embrace yours and live your life to the fullest. That is the secret to life.

What's Most Important Is Sprinting Home

My father sprinted home. My mother sprinted home too. As leadership, training, and development consultants with their own small company, my mom and dad, at various points in my young life, traveled Monday through Friday every week. In that field, if you are not on the road, you are not earning, and if they were not earning, we were not eating. And while we had some early years with a lot of puffed rice and powdered milk for breakfast, lunch, and dinner, my father and mother worked extremely hard, and over time they built a healthy business. Amazingly, though, they were focused on their WMI, which meant they rarely missed a sporting event that included one of their five children. The day of the cross-country race, the soccer, lacrosse, or basketball game, or the tennis match, one or both of them would fly home, hustle from the airport to the gym, court, or field, often arriving seconds before the start, and then be off again on a 6:00 a.m. flight the next morning. The sacrifice mattered to me because it made me feel like I mattered to them. My father sat relatively quietly in the stands, with an occasional outburst at a referee's call, but my mother was, well . . . a bit more enthusiastic. She could be heard screaming at me at the top of her lungs anytime I touched the ball. "Great job, honey" was the standard shout-out. As a freshman in a new high school trying to figure out who I was, adjust, and make friends, my-less-than helpful nickname in the hallowed halls of Our Lady of Lourdes High School in Poughkeepsie, New York, became "Honey." But it was a small price to pay for the love and support I needed at that period in my life. The commitment to get their feet to the right place at the right time was never lost on me, even as a teenager, and it later guided me as I began my own "Cats in the Cradle"–esque song of life.

I had a five-year period while working for the NBA where, like my parents before me, I traveled Monday through Friday. I was vice president of Team Marketing and Business Operations (TeamBo, as it is known in the sports industry). Dr. Bill Sutton and I were each assigned 15 teams, to cover the league. Our job was to travel to each team, find best practices, catalog them, and share them with the rest of the league to help speed the rate of innovation and success. It was long before FaceTime existed, so I politely excused myself from business dinners and press conferences to find a quiet corner in the hallway so I could whisper goodnight to my then ten-, six-, and two-year-old princesses over the phone. I also made sure I was at all the parent-teacher conferences, the holiday chorus concerts, and anything else on the docket. My WMI is being there for moments that matter.

Interviewing for my position with the 76ers, I learned that I was working for two fathers (Josh Harris and David Blitzer) with ten children between them. They too make it to their kids' basketball, baseball, and hockey games and school plays. These shared values matter to me, guide me to my WMI, and allow me to support the working father in my office who rushes into a meeting late rather than miss his daughter's preschool "Donuts with Dad." It's why I smile to hear the working mother taking a conference call from home with *Paw Patrol* blaring in the background because her afterschool nanny unexpectedly canceled. I choose to surround myself with others who aren't afraid to sprint toward WMI.

Why did I miss the 76ers' win against the Knicks? Because Alexa was Ariel in her school play, and that was the only courtside seat I wanted. It isn't easy, though, and takes some calendar juggling. From that midmorning holiday recital (a mind-numbing, anxiety-laden time of day for any working parent, and I still have no idea who selects that hour for those events) to coaching my daughter's 6:00 p.m. basketball practice only to sprint back to the arena, I have done my best to make sure my feet are in the right place at the right time, but to be where your feet are means you have to be all there—mind, body, and soul. There is no checking your phone for scores or thinking about what's coming next. You are all in. Of the iconic sports franchises—NBA, NHL, Esports, etc.—under my supervision, there is no team I take more seriously than the Rocky Crushers, Eliza's seventh-grade basketball team. I even skipped out of NBA All-Star Weekend in Chicago a day early so I could coach the team, and my administrative assistant Denise Krieg, who has been working with me for 18 years, knows to get me out of the office *no matter what* at 5:30 p.m. so I can make their practices. None of these young ladies will be lacing up in the WNBA; this is a rec league called LFE in Yardley, Pennsylvania, that focuses on the girls and drives the right values. (It does the same for the parents—no coaching allowed from the stands!) Breaking the huddle after a time-out with the "Everybody do the Rocky Rumble" stomp is truly one of my great joys. Yes, getting back and forth to a 76ers or Devils game after one of my kids' events can be a bit harried. I cut it close. I speed. I white-knuckle it on occasion as I am literally sprinting back to work, and I wouldn't want it any other way.

★ Grounding Principle ★

I know that I'm a better father, husband, friend, and church member because of the passion, intensity, and energy in my work life. By contrast, I'm a far better leader, manager, innovator, and entrepreneur in my career because I'm a father who coaches his daughters; because I'm a husband who commits to a date night; because I mentor and lead a young men's group at my church; and because I follow my daughters' lead and join them in community service projects. *I have a spring in my step you might notice if we meet when I am living my WMI.* And when I arrive somewhere, I am present, full, and devoted . . . even though I may be a few minutes late and a little breathless.

What's Most Important Is Faith

A perfect example of a family focused on their WMI is that of Vai Sikahema, a former standout football player for Brigham Young University (BYU) and in the NFL for the Arizona Cardinals and Philadelphia Eagles who is now a well-known morning news anchor on NBC 10 in Philadelphia. In 1961, Vai's parents were married on the small island of Tonga, the place they were born and raised and had never left. As devout members of the Church of Jesus Christ of Latter-day Saints, it was important for them to have their marriage "sealed." This religious ordinance bonds families for all eternity, meaning they will live together in the afterlife. It might be hard for people from another faith to understand, but its importance and meaning for those in LDS is akin to Muslims making a pilgrimage to Mecca and is something to which members of the church aspire. The sealing can only take place in a holy temple, but unfortunately, the nearest temple to Vai's parents' home was 1,500 miles away in New Zealand. A trip there was well beyond their means, yet they never lost sight of WMI.

"Despite my parents diligently saving their meager earnings, it required more," Vai explains. "They got creative, grew a huge garden, and began selling produce out of our home. When I was as young as four years old, my job was to sort melons by size to prepare for sale. Even that, though, wasn't enough to pay for the trip to New Zealand. So in the early part of 1967, my parents began selling everything and anything we owned, including the wooden siding from our small clapboard home." Neighbors bought the wood to seal their roofs, complete their own siding, or do other home projects on a tiny island where wood was at a premium. Vai's parents had finally found a currency to help save enough to be able to fulfill their WMI vision. When they left for New Zealand almost nine months later, two entire sides of their home were missing. "My parents' extraordinary faith, obedience, and drive to fulfill a vision for the future as well as their sacrifices were instilled in me and have inspired me," says Vai.

Like Vai and his parents, my WMI includes my faith, although for me this is relatively new. At 47 years old, I was baptized as a member of the Church of Jesus Christ of Latter-day Saints. This conversion came at a time in my life where I was everywhere and nowhere. My career was growing and our family unit was strong, but I wanted more . . . more connection, more grounding, more humility, and more eternal upside. When I was a child, my family went to church relatively regularly, and I had developed a strong Catholic faith. I was baptized and confirmed at our local parish, St. Patrick's in Newburgh, New York. I graduated from a Catholic high school, Our Lady of Lourdes, which provided an incredible foundation of faith and the love of the gospel, and I even graduated from a Catholic college, Villanova University.

My wife, however, was born into and lived a devoted life in the church sometimes colloquially (and incorrectly) referred to as the Mormon Church. When we decided to get married, we had several conversations about our future. I wanted the flexibility to ambitiously chase a career in sports, and I needed understanding, support, and patience, as that meant staying on the East Coast. In other words, I did not want to be pressured into moving back to her home state of Utah. Lisa quickly agreed, as she had a much tighter handle on her WMI and a much longer lens than I did. She wanted a commitment that I would support her faith and raise our future children in the church. With neither of us having a nickel to our names, that was our version of a prenup.

Lisa led our family spiritually for the first 20 years of our marriage, and I would go for a third of the three-hour church service on Sundays, as well as participate in scripture study and family home evenings each week. (These evenings are part of the culture of the church. Traditionally on Monday nights, family home evenings are a time to strengthen family ties with a lesson and activity—and if life is good some cookies. The church is centered in and around the family, and this dedicated time to talk, play games, engage each other, and stay connected—in a way, to be where your feet are—is something we do to stay together.) We tithed 10 percent of our earnings, and our girls were baptized and remain active members in the church.

Many people ask what moved me to convert after almost two decades in and around the church. I know they are looking for the Hollywood version, where I get struck by an epiphany like a lightning bolt. However, it was more about a series of moments. It's analogous to the story of pounding a huge rock over and over, a thousand times—it's not that last hit that causes it to break apart, but all the hits before it.

While Lisa never pushed me to be baptized, my children did. Alexa took great joy in telling me, "Daddy, I'm getting married in the Temple and you won't be there to see it." As a non-member of the church, it was true, I would not have been able to attend Alexa's wedding ceremony. She was just teasing, of course, but sometimes, in my moments of peaceful reflection—on a late flight delayed on the runway, in the car on the way home after a hard workout, or sitting quietly on the beach—I would think about how difficult it would be not to have that *Father of the Bride* moment. So, yes, she got to me. That said, a decision to be baptized into another faith is a lot deeper than missing a wedding, even if she is my firstborn. My other two daughters, Kira and Eliza, would take their concerns to their mother when they struggled, had questions, or were confused. One example is when they heard their Sunday school classmates talk of being "sealed" to their families; Kira and Eliza wondered what would happen to them and me. Lisa explained that I would be there for them when it counts in this life or the next.

Timing is everything, and the world is filled with what my good friend Brian Blair calls universe moments, which is when things happen for a reason and people, places, and events seemingly drop into your life with purpose. The opening of the Philadelphia Temple was one of those universe moments. The yearlong celebration brought my family closer, and definitely provided more time to reflect on my faith and how I wanted to live. We were given an open-house tour led by none other than Vai, and as I walked behind him, I had this indescribable feeling that this beautiful building was a holy place, somewhere I wanted to spend more time. Vai is not one for subtlety, nor is he one to let an opportunity pass.

"Each of your daughters will be married in this room, and we will be here together to see it," he whispered in my ear as we entered the Celestial Room. *I get it. If I convert to this church, I will be there to see my daughters married; if I don't, I won't.* We hugged. We cried. Another touch point, another moment, another opportunity to reflect on the life I was living and the life I wanted to live.

Fast-forward six months, and I had just come home from a ten-day whirlwind Miami-Vegas-NY-LA trip. It was the summer and I was tired of traveling, longing to get back to the routine of the fall, and feeling a bit empty as Lisa and the girls were still away. *I'm ready to be baptized* was the prompting that kept coming into my head. Was it real? Or was it just me missing my family and being exhausted from travel? The only way to find the answer is to "do the work," as I am fond of saying in the office. Nothing in this world is free, and important answers to important questions do not pop out of thin air. In this case, I was committed to doing the necessary work to pressure test my prompting. I was reading *The Book of Mormon Miracle* by a dear family friend, Randal Wright, who inspired me to write this book. I was listening to scriptures in the mornings on my phone and a talk a day from one of the Church leaders that Lisa was texting into our family group chat. And I was praying more than usual, asking for guidance and strength and giving thanks for all my blessings. The more work I did, the more convinced I became that the time was now.

Out to dinner at Red Sombrero, a down-home Mexican restaurant in Kennett Square, Pennsylvania, with Clark Maxwell, my spiritual guide and our family's home teacher, I got right to it. (Your "home teacher" is somebody assigned from the church to check in with your family once a month to see what you need or teach a lesson. Clark had been ours for three years.)

"I want to be baptized," I told him. "And I want to know how we get this done quickly and quietly." Clark answered my questions, all with an ear-to-ear smile, and set up the first meeting with the missionaries later that night. (Missionaries are 18- to 21-year-old young men and women who take a pause from their secular life to go teach and preach the gospel. Part of the conversion process is their teaching.)

I knew I was ready. This faith had become WMI.

When Lisa and the girls returned from their trip, I asked Lisa to come into the living room. I closed the doors behind us. We sat across from each other, and I held her hands and told her I loved her and had something I wanted to tell her.

"I've been meeting with Clark and the missionaries because I've decided it's time to get baptized."

"Wait, what?" she kept saying. "Seriously? Is this for real?" she asked over and over. We cried and hugged for quite some time. It was a special moment that I will cherish forever. That night, I sent hundreds of texts to those who had provided me moments, friendship, and influence on my journey. I announced my intention to be baptized with a Bitmoji of me dressed like a missionary with the phrase "I Believe" scrawled across the top and the time, date, and place of my baptism. Friends came from all over the country to attend, and we threw one heck of a party at our house afterward to celebrate.

★ **Grounding Principle** ★

The church is both a grounding and guiding center for my WMI. Today, as the world moves faster and there seems to be more chaos than calm, *it's likely worth exploring your own centering force—whether that's faith, church, prayer, meditation, running, yoga, or anything else that helps enhance your level of peace, increase your level of calm, and provide a more centered life.*

What's Most Important Is Health

Another story that highlights WMI is that of McCall Reynolds, my niece through marriage to my nephew Josh. To know McCall is to love her for her dry sense of humor, passion for adventure, and charming style. Their wedding took place at the Provo City Center Temple followed by an all-out, let-your-hair-down reception complete with dancing, music, and lots and lots of cake. It was a fun and festive way to celebrate the start of married life for a young couple who were so committed and in love, surrounded by all those who matter in their lives.

McCall looked even more striking than usual on her wedding day, but she didn't seem particularly happy or feel much like herself. She seemed distracted when her guests gushed over her dress, and she tripped over her own feet during her first dance with Josh. She continued to feel "off" (her word) during her honeymoon, passive where she had once been full of life. When the newlyweds returned, McCall went to see her doctor, and while the initial tests didn't find anything, she knew something just wasn't right. She insisted the next doctor order a CAT scan, which revealed a tangerine-size tumor in McCall's frontal lobe. Josh's text in our family group chat said it all: "Bad news. McCall has a tumor. Surgery tomorrow. We could use some prayers. Love you guys, Josh." Prior to her eight-hour emergency surgery at the University of Utah, the 24-year-old newlywed was encouraged to make any final adjustments to her will and "get her affairs in order." Sometimes life throws you curveballs, and sometimes life isn't fair. And this was one of those times. Sometimes we are reminded that WMI includes the simple things that we haven't considered before, like health. A 24-year-old shouldn't have to get her affairs in order. She's too young. She has too much to look forward to.

While McCall was in surgery, I was pacing the sidelines of our empty Philadelphia 76ers Training Complex court, on a call with a colleague, heatedly debating a recent deal that had gone south in a surprising hurry. While it was a distraction from the gravity of what was happening to my niece two thousand miles away, I was hoping it wasn't a harbinger of things to come. The night before, after an infamous and excruciating three-year rebuilding "process" for the 76ers, we won the right to select the No. 1 draft pick in the 2016 NBA Draft Lottery. We would eventually select Ben Simmons, who would become Rookie of the Year, make multiple All-Star teams, and, with Joel Embiid, become part of the most dynamic young duo in the NBA. Both were heading for superstardom, and the team was headed for a lot more wins. Two days before that, we had announced the first jersey patch partnership in U.S. professional sports, complete with an international media tour during which I had given dozens of interviews. It was emotional and mental overload as we felt the tide beginning to turn in favor of our team after years of swimming against it. Google "76ers the Process" if you aren't familiar with that period in the team's history. The world was waking up to this little experiment as we were actually getting some momentum. A bit of good news was a welcome relief, but it wasn't the relaxing kind of relief; instead, it shifted us into overdrive. Our sales call centers were receiving inbound calls as late as 1:00 a.m., and most of the 76ers staff were working around the clock, some choosing to spend the night at the office. I hadn't slept in days for a different reason; I couldn't shake the image of a tumor the size of a tangerine in McCall's brain.

★ Grounding Principle ★

As I paced and paced, I got a text message from Josh. Irritated and exasperated by what I was dealing with on my conference call but unable to properly put it in perspective, I muted the call to open the text. It was a picture of McCall on a bed in the recovery room wearing a 76ers t-shirt. A longtime fan, she held up one finger in the air. Josh had captioned the photo: "McCall came out of surgery and her first question was, 'Did we get the No. 1 Pick?'" Instantly, I was slapped back to reality—*true* reality. I was standing ten steps away from our head coach Brett Brown's office. His famed Bostralian accent ran through my mind, saying "WMI." He'd had it printed on the top of every notepad in our training complex.

WMI . . . What's most important? Family and love. All that stress over a deal gone south, media interviews, the staff working around the clock, mounting losses, and a rotating door of executives and players had been put in check, a reality check, because nothing matters unless we have our health, because that is WMI.

What's Most Important Is Preparing Our Children to Thrive in Our Changing World

I vividly remember as a young father trying to figure out parenthood (it's a never-ending process) and a three-year-old Alexa throwing her dinner on the floor piece by piece. As I sternly told her, "Please stop" and "No, Alexa," she clenched her fist and punched me square in the jaw. I always said I wanted tough daughters, but this wasn't exactly what I had in mind. Yet that was Alexa as a young child, adolescent, and teen. She was like her dad—a roller-coaster of emotions and very tough. Fast-forward to last summer, when Alexa, nineteen at the time, accompanied me to a friend's wedding in

Athens, just the two of us. She had been there the previous summer, working at a Syrian refugee camp, and was excited to show me around. The first place she took me to was the youth hostel where she'd lived.

"There it is," she said, pointing to a building with barred windows surrounded by abandoned buildings and seedy characters. (It was like New York City's Hell's Kitchen in the 1980s, if that means anything to you.)

"Alexa, you lived here?" I asked, having had no idea how tough the neighborhood was. "This seems really dangerous."

"It was dangerous, but not as dangerous as the subway I took to work," she said.

"Really?"

"Yes, but wait till you see the refugee camp—now that was really dangerous," she replied nonchalantly, explaining to me that the people at the camp were the lucky ones compared to those who were squatters and those living on the street. "At least those in the refugee camps had a place to live with their families."

"Did you ever feel unsafe?" I asked, now anxiously questioning the fact that I'd signed off on her living there the previous year without really checking into it.

"I can handle myself, Dad," she replied. *Whoa.* But I was not surprised. I felt a sense of relief that Alexa was okay and a sense of pride that she'd become this strong woman. Working in that refugee camp had been important enough for her to push through because she found meaning in what she was doing. She'd found her WMI.

Sometimes life lessons come when you least expect them, while other times, when you are in the company of extraordinary leaders, parents, coaches, and people, it is best to just ask questions, listen, learn, and take notes. I often feel that way when I am around my long-time friend Henry Johnson, who is the president of Northern Trust. He is a brilliant leader and looks like the Hollywood 1940s version of the part: tall, blonde, handsome, and impeccably dressed. There is just something about him that makes everyone in the room stop when he enters. He has an important job, but I am more interested in learning how he parents his three sons than his latest read on the stock market. He always seems so balanced, directed, and composed, whereas I can feel like I am in the eye of a hurricane with my three daughters—surrounded by a vortex of teenage angst, basketball practice woes, and wardrobe issues. We were in his Midtown Manhattan corner office, where it seemed like you could see the entire city through the windows. We were chatting about our children, and I was carrying on about one of my daughters leaving her clothes everywhere. It was delivered with a bent of humor, but it was on my mind enough to mention. I was saying that the volume of clothes they throw on the floor amazes me, and it's as if the girls change four times a day and in all corners of the house—the kitchen, my bathroom, the family room, and even in my car. Henry's gentle smile hardened, and he sternly stared me down.

"If that is the biggest issue you are having with your teenage daughters, you should stop and count your blessings," he said. "Take a breath and appreciate what you have. Second, if there are clothes on the ground, pick them up. To have that turn your mood or be on your mind enough to be talking about it with me is not a good use of your energy. Lastly, I imagine there are so many things you want to talk to your daughters about before they head off to college. Time is precious, and you need to treat it better. Choose your moments and words more carefully. Focus on the big rocks and allocate them wisely." Gulp. Good point, Henry, and another reminder to focus on WMI.

Of course, most times, it's hard to discern if our efforts with our children are even noticed, and the more stressed we are by work and life, the easier it can be to give up on the seemingly little connections that mean a great deal. Don't. Keep doing what you are doing and trust your instincts. My friend Jim Fiore, senior vice president of Wheels Up, explained it best to me with this next story. When his son Michael was young, Jim struggled to be where his feet are at home. During Michael's elementary school years, Jim would write a note in Sharpie marker on the outside of Michael's brown paper lunch bag. Sometimes it was a quote, other times a personal note of inspiration and love. He also made it a point to see him off to school at the bus stop each morning and pick him up every afternoon. (His assistant was under explicit instructions to clear his schedule from 2:45 to 3:30 p.m. so he was free to do this. His calendar was blocked, and it was his WMI.)

After Jim and his wife separated, he moved to a neighboring town. To continue his brown bag message routine, he'd wake up 45 minutes early and quickly get ready so he could drive to his ex-wife's house and write the notes for his son. While running late on a cold, blustery February morning, Jim pushed the speed limit and slid off the slick, icy road into a ditch. He wasn't hurt, but his car was dented, and the ensuing tow truck delay caused him to miss his opportunity to see Michael off to school and write his lunch bag message for the day.

"Feeling angry and sorry for myself, I became convinced that the whole brown bag note tradition was futile—a total waste of time. What was I doing making myself crazy and getting into car accidents? Just so I could write a note on a lunch bag?" Jim says. "I bet Michael didn't even read them and most likely didn't quite understand them anyway, I thought." Jim still did his best to be at the bus stop each morning and afternoon, but the brown bag notes became a thing of the past. One day, Jim arrived for pickup earlier than normal. Instead of waiting at the bus stop, he decided to do a load of Michael's laundry. Afterward, he took the freshly folded clothes upstairs to Michael's room and began putting them into his bureau.

"I was just about finished when I opened the final drawer," Jim explains. "What I observed left me speechless and numb. Michael had saved *every single* brown bag on which I had written the notes. He'd come home and placed them in a safe place. They were crumpled and squeezed into that bottom drawer like sardines into a can. I dropped to my knees and cried uncontrollably."

★ Grounding Principle ★

"It hit me all at once: the love I had for this child and his impact on me. The evidence was there in all those saved brown paper bags," Jim says. "I felt my purpose as a father take hold, and I felt, too, that I had taken the initial step down a long road to full strength. In those brown bags, I had found hope, reengaged faith, and rekindled the feeling of love." Jim had rediscovered his WMI.

The bottom line when it comes to WMI is to *figure out what is critical and core in your life.* This reminds me of Rahim Thompson, who was born with a hearing impairment and spent parts of his childhood homeless and living in a car. He is now best known for running one of the most competitive high school basketball leagues in the country, located in Philadelphia, the

Chosen League, which began as an outdoor league played at the Cherashore Playground. In fact, ESPN highlighted it as one of the best outdoor leagues in the country. Rahim had come up with the idea and was planning the details when his apartment was robbed and then his beloved grandmother passed away. He was devastated and unsure he'd continue with the endeavor. After the funeral, Rahim's godmother spoke with him and told him it was very important to her that he take a leadership role in his community. "That motivated me to do the league even more," Rahim explains. "I'd been robbed, but I couldn't quit." In 2002, he used his paycheck from a job at the Parking Authority as funding and slept on his godmother's couch. When he lost his job, he *still* didn't give up on the league. In fact, he was even more determined and worked around the clock to find sponsors.

Today, it's one of the few high school leagues in the country to have several major sponsors. Almost 150 alums of the program have played Division 1 in college, and some of these are names you would know from the NBA, such as Kyle Kuzma, Kyle Lowry, Marcus Morris, and Dion Waiters, among others. I am fortunate to call Rahim a friend. I admire him for what he's done for over a thousand kids who have gone to college on athletic scholarships and for the fact that he's an influential guy in the world of high school basketball in Philadelphia. But more than that, I admire him because he has his WMI in clear focus. Rahim shines around the holidays as the memory of him growing up without pushes him to help others. On Thanksgiving he provides the holiday dinner that he never had to other families, and on Christmas he gives the presents that he never received to kids who otherwise might not get them. His WMI is helping others who may be where he was and honoring the dream his mother, grandmother, and godmother all had for him to become a leader in his community. He has done that in spades.

Rahim has a beautiful family, and he never forgot where he came from or what it means to struggle. *So what matters more than anything else to* you? *These are your guideposts*, and any moment spent away from them is likely not a good use of time, a wasted effort, or, worse yet, just noise. This applies to work, home, faith, family, health, friends, and community. Your WMI might change, and it might be different for you today than three years from now, and it might be different for you at home or with your spouse or with good friends or when coaching a team. But you've got to figure out what the main thing is and transfer the time, energy, resources, and mindshare there. Put the emphasis where it belongs, in your WMI, and the rewards you will reap are hard to put into words. Your focus will be clearer, your goals will be easier to achieve, and the people in your life who are WMI will feel that they matter, deepening your connection. What could be better than that?

What's Most Important Is
Valuing Equality

But we can't just have our own personal WMI. We need to have a WMI as a community, a country, and the world. Nothing brought this into the spotlight more than the pandemic and national protests in the spring of 2020. I don't know about you, but to me it felt like the world was falling apart. Human dignity matters more than anything, and if we don't have that basic building block, then what do we have? I learned so much about this during that time—or maybe I should say, I learned how much I *didn't* know. I grew up in a diverse neighborhood. I considered myself comfortable with, knowledgeable about, and an ally of diverse groups—I considered myself "woke." But boy did I have a lot to learn . . .

In July of 2020, our company had a virtual Zoom forum for Black and Brown members of our staff to share their experience of racism and bias. What was supposed to last an hour became two, and it was heavy. *Heavy.* There were so many eye-opening, stunning, heartbreaking stories that left many of us in tears, even more of us learning how little we knew, and all of us committing to learn more and do more.

The first one was from Elton Brand, the general manager of the 76ers. One night he accidentally tripped the security alarm in his home in Villanova, a beautiful Philadelphia suburb. When he heard the cop cars coming, he asked his wife, Seneca, to go greet them at the door. "Why? You were the one who tripped the alarm," she said. But Elton said that's just not how it works.

"If they see a six-foot-eight Black man coming out of a house in this neighborhood, I will be on the pavement with my hands behind my back, handcuffed before they ask me what my name is," Elton explained. I was stunned. Elton Brand is one of the most recognizable people in Philadelphia, in the top five for sure. He's been in the public eye as a player, has made millions in his career, and he's a GM in the NBA, one of the most powerful positions in sports, and yet *that's* his reality? He continued by sharing a story about getting pulled over while driving his Tesla. Immediately, he put his hands out the window so the cop would see them when he walked over to the car. "Hey, *you're* Elton Brand," the cop said when he approached. *Phew,* he thought. *Thank God, I'm Elton Brand.* Who knows what could have happened if he hadn't been recognized? I've been pulled over several times and never had that fear.

Sadly, Elton is not alone. This is a common theme for African American males. "Even when I go jogging in my neighborhood, I wear a protective vest because I don't want people to think, *Who is this big black guy running in my neighborhood?*" Elton explained. It's something he has to think about all the time, which is why we have to change our thinking too. This doesn't sound like equality. This doesn't feel like equality. This isn't equality. We can do better.

Desron Dorset, vice president of business development for the Philadelphia 76ers, also talked about being pulled over in his BMW about 50 times. Yes, he admits that he drives too fast, but that's not the biggest issue. "Almost 40 of those 50 times I've been asked, 'Is this your car?'" Desron explained. Then he looked straight into the Zoom camera and said, "Scott, how many times have *you* been asked if it's your car when you've been pulled over?" Whoa. I had no words. My heart sank, and no, I'd never been asked if it was my car. This doesn't feel like equality either.

The third person was Lexi Williams, a young sales rep for the New Jersey Devils, who went to prep school, attended a predominantly white college, and now lives in Hoboken, New Jersey, in an upscale neighborhood where she says no one looks like her. When it was her turn to talk during the forum, she began with, "I want to share a very isolated story to show every white person why your voice does matter." She talked about having to move her car because there is alternate-side-of-the-street parking in her neighborhood, and she didn't want her car to get towed.

"I went downstairs in a black t-shirt and a pair of old shorts I've had since the tenth grade. As soon as I reached my doorstep, I realized that I was not dressed to move my car. What does being dressed to move your car look like?" she asked. "I never go outside without wearing something that looks like I belong in my neighborhood or could be visiting someone in my neighborhood—a Lululemon or New Jersey Devils shirt. I never wear something that doesn't say, 'Hey, I fit in here.'"

That morning, she didn't think those old running shorts fit the bill.

"I decided to move my car anyway, but I was terrified," she explained. "I ran to my car, but when I got there, I realized I needed to slow down. If I approached my own car too fast, I thought, it would look like I was stealing it. Once I started to drive, all I could think of was my 'alibi.' If I get pulled over . . . if something happens in the two blocks I need to move my car, what would I say to a police officer who pulls me over? I need to be rehearsed. I need to make it sound believable. 'I'm moving my car. I'm not doing anything wrong.' My brain and the society I live in has taught me to think like this." Another gut punch and reality check for those of us who are white and can just go downstairs and move our cars. When Lexi posted this story online, she ended it by saying, "So, at the very least, you can use your voice. Please understand that, on a micro-level, you are making it so that I feel OK walking outside in non-name-brand items so that no one calls the police and so I don't die."

I needed to get educated. I started reading *White*

Fragility and a Harvard Business School case study on systemic racism in the United States. I watched movies like *Just Mercy*, *13th*, and a documentary about the Tulsa Race Massacre. This was the start of my reeducation. I needed to learn more, read more, study more, and listen more. We had other open forums at work and listened to more stories about racism and growing up Black in America. The more we learned, the more we became convinced that we had to do something. Fortunately, I work for Josh Harris, David Blitzer, and Michael Rubin, three partners who are committed to leveraging their platforms for good and want to be leaders in diversity and inclusion. Josh invests with After-School All-Stars, David with DREAM (formerly Harlem RBI), and Michael set up the REFORM Alliance to help those who are unjustly imprisoned. At HBSE, our plan of action includes committing $20 million by and through:

- APPOINTING LEADERSHIP. HBSE will create a new team, led by a chief diversity and impact officer to spearhead internal and external diversity and inclusion standards, programs, and initiatives across the organization.
- INVESTING IN BLACK COMMUNITIES. HBSE is committed to community development efforts that revitalize the neighborhoods where its teams and fans are located. Through

partnerships with Black developers, local community groups, and officials, *HBSE Real Estate's Community Advancement Program* will advance equitable, community-driven revitalization through significant investments.

- SUPPORTING BLACK-OWNED BUSINESSES AND ENTREPRENEURS. Consistent with its dedication to fostering the entrepreneurial spirit, HBSE will implement new initiatives to support Black-owned businesses with competitive opportunities and marketing resources.

- PROMOTING EDUCATION, HEALTH, AND EMPLOYMENT. HBSE will commit $2.5 million through the *Sixers Youth Foundation* and *Devils Care Foundation*, continuing to work through their Corporate Responsibility programs to support positive education, health, and employment outcomes in Black communities. This commitment builds upon efforts made by HBSE to promote racial equity in Newark, Camden, and Philadelphia.

- AMPLIFYING A WORKPLACE OF RESPECT, INCLUSION, AND DIVERSITY. HBSE is dedicated to supporting Black and minority executives entering and ascending in the sports and entertainment industry and fostering a diverse and inclusive workplace through recruitment, dynamic partnerships, and programs

that provide support and enrichment opportunities for all employees and athletes.

This is just the beginning, and it isn't nearly
enough. Several season ticket holders canceled their
tickets because of our commitment to Black Lives
Matter, social justice, and championing equality.
What? But doesn't everyone deserve an equal shot
in America? The American dream? Equality is my
WMI. So is learning, and so is making a difference.
It's time for change, and I hope these season ticket
holders commit to learning, reading, and educating
themselves. And to tell you the truth, I'm not interested in seeing them in the arena until they do.
It's time to get on the right side of history. This has
nothing to do with politics; this has everything to do
with humanity.

⨍ Your Turn to Put This into Practice ⨍

Identify three things that are your WMI. Keep this list
visible as a daily reminder to consciously spend your
precious time where it belongs.

WMI

1.
2.
3.

Next, since time is finite, engage in a *Start, Stop, Continue* exercise so you can most effectively focus on the following:

Three things I am not doing that I should start doing to contribute to my WMI:

1.
2.
3.

Three things I am going to stop doing so I can focus more on my WMI:

1.
2.
3.

Three things I am doing that I should continue doing so I can continue to put emphasis on my WMI:

1.
2.
3.

CHAPTER 4

Fail Forward

Smooth seas do not make for skillful sailors.
—African proverb

Failure is a more effective teacher than success. It doesn't mean it is enjoyable; it isn't. However, failing is a critical piece in your development and learning as a student of life. That means you must identify and compartmentalize the lessons learned from a failure, a process that I call failing forward (versus failing backward). Because without learning from failure, your inner voice—the one in your head whispering around every decision, meeting, or opportunity—will take a turn for the worse and tell you that you are not good enough, smart enough, or talented enough. This happened to me.

It was 1988, and I was an overconfident high school senior excitedly awaiting my acceptance letters from the eight colleges to which I applied. I was a straight-A student, president of the student body, captain of three sports teams, even president of the local National Honor Society chapter. And I had even recently been featured on an ESPN show called *Scholastic Sports America*. While I was on the lower end of the acceptance range of SAT scores for my target schools, I thought I was a lock to get into most of them. The short walk down the driveway became a lot longer on the way back up as rejection letter after rejection letter arrived. Stretch schools like Princeton University and Stanford University came pretty fast: "We are sorry to inform you . . ." But I never made it past the first line. Then the dark clouds rolled in from my top two choices, the University of Notre Dame and Georgetown University, where I was waitlisted and eventually rejected. Ouch. I was devastated, and the impact was indelible. *I am not smart enough*, I thought. Even today, as I type, I still feel a pinch of emotion, embarrassment, and frustration.

In the end, I was fortunately accepted into two colleges, Syracuse University and Villanova University. Two of eight. Not exactly what I was expecting, but I chose to become a Villanova Wildcat. While I know now that failure is a much better teacher than success, my takeaway as an 18-year-old was that I wasn't smart enough; it left a giant chip on my shoulder that would take years to knock off. In some cases it was the fuel I needed, and in others it was a really bad use of energy. I knew that self-pity and whining did not constitute a strategy, so I went on a mission to prove to the world or maybe just myself that I was smart. I may have been the only student at Villanova to go multiple semesters without missing a class, and I was usually the nerd sitting in the front row and more than occasionally raising my hand. On purpose? Yes. I took two calculus electives. I took 12 credits of Japanese electives. (Yes, 12!) On purpose, again. Nobody knew, nobody cared, except for me, of course, trying to silence the inner monologue. The one and only ancillary benefit that came from my internal battle was that somewhere along the way I fell in love with learning, something that became a lifelong pursuit and my new source of fuel. Ah, at last, a lesson learned.

Fast-forward eight years and I was 26 years old, a director of corporate sales with the Philadelphia Eagles, newly married to Lisa (who had a heck of a trajectory in the sports business too), and, for the first time, making enough money to pay the rent and go out to dinner on occasion, thinking perhaps I had "made it." After two years I was excelling in sponsorship sales, "making it rain" as it were, but I was failing miserably as a first-time manager. I had ambitions to be a team president and was aware the job description started with "manager" and ended with "leader." It was time to get some professional training, so I explored going back to school to get my MBA. This time, though, instead of blanketing the country with applications, I submitted only one, to Harvard Business School (HBS), and was accepted. But, as Lisa and I packed up our black VW Jetta and headed north toward Cambridge, Massachusetts, I became increasingly worried that I couldn't live up to the challenge. That inner voice still occupied as much real estate in my mind as the chip on my shoulder.

It is hard to describe the raw humility I felt upon arrival at Harvard Business School's campus that January. Lisa was on the job hunt, and I decided to brave the classically bitter Boston cold and walk from our tiny apartment to the student center. It was lunchtime on day one, and I bought a sandwich and some hot chocolate and sat at an empty table. Self-doubt began to creep into my head. *What am I doing here? I had a cool job with the Philadelphia Eagles. I loved our life.* This loop of negative thoughts was broken by two people—one woman and one man—sitting down next to me.

"What did you do for work before you came here?" I asked each of them, breaking the awkward silence. This was the standard day one question.

"I was working for BCG helping the Russian government restructure their economy," the woman replied. *BC . . . what? What the heck am I doing here?* The gentleman answered that he was running a private equity firm, his "family office." Not knowing at the time that a family office is what very wealthy people set up to manage their money, I naively replied, "That's great, my parents are entrepreneurs." He just smiled. Turns out his last name is Liechtenstein . . . as in the country of Liechtenstein. *Wait, what?*

I was surrounded by people who seemed to be both smarter and more competent, and who had better and more relevant experience. Having spent my short career tied up in sports, my first instinct was to compete with them. I'd outwork them, outscore them, run 'em into the ground. After two weeks, even I could see that this was a failed strategy, as I was feeling increasingly isolated and overworked, and I was performing at a mediocre level at best. I felt exposed. I was anxious walking into class, dreading the HBS "cold call" from the professor to an unsuspecting student at the start of each class. I was "gripping the stick too tight," as they say in hockey.

Dean Kim Clark, my professors, the administrators, and even my classmates were all saying the same thing, over and over: "Look around, these are your friends. Help each other today, help each other tomorrow . . . there will be no better network in the world than the one you have in this classroom." The narrative continued: "When someone from Harvard calls, you pick up the phone and help. That is what we do. This is who we are." After a while, the sheer logic of having nine hundred friends—who were from all over the world, in every discipline, and all outstanding—to call on through the course of a career sounded like a can't-lose proposition.

I finally got it. My sports translation: This is not golf, this is a team sport. This is basketball. Be a teammate. That sounded like a better game, and it was one I felt much more comfortable playing. Over time, I began to relax, laugh, listen, and prepare to learn. At HBS we were put in the same classroom in the same seat with the same people for six months. This created a laboratory in which to learn, and as I learned, I grew as a person and made lifelong friends.

At one point, I had a final coming up in managerial finance. Worried about it, I went to meet with the professor.

"I'm anxious about the final," I told him.

"Get out your pen and paper and write this down," he said. Ready with pen in hand, I waited for my professor to continue talking.

"It's better to have more money than less money," my professor said. "Got that?"

I nodded as I wrote it down.

"It's better to have that money sooner than later," he went on.

"Okay," I said as I continued to write.

"Scott, are you going to be a CEO someday?"

"Yes," I said.

"The final thing to write down: Hire a great CFO," he said.

"This isn't going to help for the final tomorrow, is it?" I asked, finally getting it.

"Nope," he said. "But you're going to be just fine." This perfectly summarizes HBS: the environment is about learning how to be the next great CEO and creating lifelong relationships—it's *not* about grades. It was a different mentality. No ceilings, a newfound family, and limitless dreams . . . and the people I met there *did* change my life. As the walls we built as defense systems came tumbling down, I realized that everyone felt vulnerable and uncomfortable. It was clear that, other than a few trained consultants from Bain, BCG, and McKinsey who could formulate any case into a client-facing model as they would in their former lives, success was intermittent for the rest of us. A third of my classmates spoke English as a second language. The idea of me going to China, learning Mandarin, and engaging in a business school discussion seemed like a tall mountain to think about, let alone climb. And that was the norm, as my classmates hailed from all over the world. I had so much respect for them, and it was also a pretty humbling experience. And the love of learning I had gained at Villanova extended to the HBS curriculum. Over time, I gained confidence in my skill set where it was strongest (for instance, I was good at talking in front of groups and had experience in high-stress environments), and I learned to ask for help when I was lost (for instance, when valuing a company for sale or doing any financial analysis). The latter was truly a gift and another lesson as I continued to fail forward.

★ Grounding Principle ★

Two years after I arrived at Harvard, I was selected by my peers to speak at graduation to the nine hundred graduates of the HBS class of 1998 and our families. As I looked out over the sea of people, I smiled, thinking of the mountain we had climbed and the peaks ahead that we, as a class, would summit. I had compartmentalized my insecurities, worked hard, and bloomed where I was planted. I was more appreciative than ever of Professor Failure, who had taught me more than I could ever learn on my own: *Stop competing, stop pressing so hard, and start opening yourself up to people and learning. Stop trying to prove what you know and begin to express that you're intellectually curious. Be interested versus interesting.*

Being Effective Is More Important Than Being Right

Every once in a while, you are in the right place at the right time with the right person, you receive sound counsel, and you actually listen. This happened to me about six months into my rocky start at the NBA. I was vice president of Team Marketing and Business Operations (TMBO), and I was walking into NBA HR chief Jeff Robinson's office for my six-month new employee review. I was armed with detailed reports identifying my efforts and vision in the NBA's newest department, one that commissioner David Stern had stacked with a crack team of executives to build the McKinsey & Co. of sports that would identify, amplify, and share best practices to drive higher performance across teams. I also was ready to complain. A lot. I had never worked at a big company before, and I was finding it virtually impossible to accomplish anything.

The onboarding experience had been rough, as the group was ill prepared for me. At the three-month mark, I had no laptop (so I brought mine from home), no business cards (this wasn't great when meeting people on the road), and no office phone number (now that was a challenge). These were all inconvenient and frustrating, but I could work through them. *Maybe this was just how it was in big companies*, I thought. Unfortunately, there was one thing that was more than an inconvenience: after three months of travel, I had amassed $30,000 in expenses, and I could not get approval or reimbursement, which sent my wife and me further and further into the debt we began when HoopsTV crashed just months earlier. On top of this, unbeknownst to me, a well-entrenched NBA executive had slowed all my progress to a halt. This person had spent an entire career at the NBA while I was an overconfident 29-year-old with a job title that she felt was out of whack for my age and experience. I felt stifled and frustrated, and I was not having fun for the first time in my professional life. I didn't know what to do or how to handle it. Jeff suggested I approach my boss with the issues and challenges. I did, and by that afternoon I had an office (I had been working at a desk recently vacated by an intern), business cards, a phone, and a reimbursement check for my expenses. As frustrating as these challenges were, I had a much bigger problem . . . and it was me.

I thought I had applied my traditional "team player" strategy. When the Women's National Basketball Association (WNBA) was struggling, I dove in headfirst. The theory at the time was that the brand needed to appeal more strongly to teenage girls, so following a consultation with Val Ackerman, who ran the league and her WNBA marketing team, and through a relationship I had, we created what I thought was an unbelievable partnership and brand campaign with NSYNC, a boy band led by Justin Timberlake that was exploding in popularity. We gave out autographed merchandise, signed major radio stations as promotional partners, and launched NSYNC's album at halftime of a WNBA game. And guess what? It failed miserably. Attendance did not increase at all. This was almost impossible, because anything NSYNC touched went through the roof and was a wild success. *How could this possibly fail? Why am I failing?* I wondered.

But as I sat in Jeff's office, armed with a quiver of arrows and a dozen targets throughout the company, I still had not put it together: I was the problem.

"How's it going?" he asked.

"Terribly," I said. "I can't get anything done. Nobody moves here. It's like they are working against me. I'm a salmon swimming upstream. This place is awful."

"What role do you think you are playing in your own demise?" Jeff said, shaking his head.

"Me? Are you serious? I'm jumping in and helping people who do not want help and are not interested in success." I was confused, to say the least.

"How many days do you spend on the road?" he asked.

"Five. Well, on average. Counting weekend games?" I asked proudly.

"You spend five days on the road and you can't get anything done at the home office? That's incredible," he said, with evident sarcasm.

"No. I don't mean that."

"Scott, when was the last time you took someone out to breakfast just to say hello and show interest? When was the last time you checked in to see if someone with NBA Entertainment could use some help with one of the teams? Have you even been to their offices across the river in Secaucus, New Jersey?" he asked, knowing the answer.

"Uh, never. I mean, I should . . ."

"You're so concerned with being right, but you seem to have little interest in being effective," said Jeff. "If you want to be effective, you have to look in the mirror and stop blaming everyone else."

"What do you mean?" I asked.

"This organization is a matrix. You need to have a relationship with someone in every box to move the needle," he explained. "What if someone had your back in marketing? What if you had a great connection with the events team? What if you met with the head of digital media for lunch every other week? Can you imagine how much faster you could move the ball here? Those programs that went dead? In the end, who is really responsible? Who is really accountable? You are!"

"I only add value on the road," I said stubbornly, but my tone indicated I had begun to doubt this.

"That's the problem. You need to add more value *here* so you can add more value on the road with *teams*. Create relationships. Offer help. Be an extraordinary teammate. Take people to lunch when you *don't* need something, check in on them *just because*, help them *before* they ask. You'll get things done if you build some equity in the office."

I listened. I reflected. I came off the road two days

a week and spent one day in our NBA Entertainment offices in Secaucus, which had the reputation of being a bit "forgotten." Being around presented an even better opportunity to connect, make friends, and drive the business. I didn't spend much time in my own office; instead, I explored other floors, met with other department heads, shared the goals of my own department, and offered my team as a resource. I learned from Jeff and shifted my mindset from interesting to being interested. "I know your time is valuable. I want to learn a bit more about your department and role here. I'm new, and I think I could learn quite a bit from understanding your department's goals, victories, and struggles, and how you like to manage, work, and communicate with others . . ." And it worked. Jeff's unbelievable insight transformed my career, and after several months I was able to build a reputation as *that* guy who could "get things done" with the teams. I found myself in meetings I had no business being in and offering advice to executives decades my senior. I was making things happen, being useful, helpful, making a difference. And I was having fun again.

★ Grounding Principle ★

A year later, in 2005, Gregg Winik, president of NBA Entertainment, was talking about our need to promote the NBA Finals. He was concerned that the ratings would be down given the lack of national interest in the qualifying teams, the Detroit Pistons and San Antonio Spurs.

"I can get the teams to help and promote the finals," I told Gregg.

"Yeah right," he scoffed, then actually laughed. "The teams never do anything like that. I bet you can't get *one*."

"We can get ten before lunch," I said, smiling more confidently than I had in some time. By noon, 15 teams had committed; by the end of the day, all 30 had come on board to leverage their radio, billboards, email, and websites to promote the NBA Finals. Why? The relationships and trust we had worked diligently to cultivate between TMBO and the NBA were now fully formed and authentic. Had I still been in my previous state, Gregg and I would never have had that conversation, and I would never have been able to engage through TMBO and coordinate with the teams. Jeff was right and effective. Teams and executives I'd supported and gone to bat for were eager to do the same for the league, and for the first time in my career, *I was focused on being effective and less concerned with being right*.

Big Platform, Small Delivery

Another one of my transformative moments of failure occurred when my boss at the NBA, Bernie Mullin, left to become the CEO of the NBA's Atlanta Hawks and the NHL's Atlanta Thrashers, vacating the highly coveted role of running TMBO. The morning after Bernie announced he was leaving, extension 8300 flashed on my office phone, a number that made my heart beat a bit faster and the room temperature rise. It was the intimidating force known as Commissioner David Stern calling. His "relentless pursuit of perfection" coupled with his two core management principles—(1) fear and intimidation are effective motivators, and (2) episodic micromanagement drives extraordinary outcomes—both inspired and terrified young leaders, myself included.

"I can't believe I'm going to *bleeping* do this, especially for someone as incompetent as you are," he said on the other end of the phone. "But you've got the job."

"Thanks," I managed to say. "For the opportunity, not for the 'incompetent' line." I think I heard him chuckle as he slammed down the phone. My new position as senior vice president of TMBO gave me a seat at the adult table and would change the trajectory of my career by exposing me to people and challenges that still impact and influence me today. A couple days later, my phone rang with that familiar extension again. I picked up the receiver quickly, before the heat could fully rise to my forehead, and heard a stream of curse words on the other end of the line.

"Hey, what's up, David?" I said nonchalantly, pretending I wasn't feeling even a pinch of anxiety.

"What's up? What's up?" he said, the volume of his voice rising. "Well, you're going to speak at the board meeting on Thursday. Don't *bleep* it up." Then he slammed the phone down. At the time, I didn't have any meaningful experience in public speaking, so I was more than a little nervous with just three days to prepare. This board meeting is the same one I attended years later as the president of Madison Square Garden Sports for the New York Knicks and still attend today as alternate governor of the Philadelphia 76ers. It is attended by most of those who have acquired teams, their lead partner, and sometimes the person running the business. Michael Jordan, Jim Dolan, Ted Leonsis, Wyc Grousbeck, Mark Cuban, Josh Harris, David Blitzer, Jeanie Buss, Dan Gilbert, Larry Tanenbaum, Wes Edens, Marc Lasry, Herb Simon . . . this is a high-powered room, a who's-who-of-the-world-type room.

As I walked into the huge, ornate ballroom on the top floor of the St. Regis Hotel in Midtown Manhattan, David beelined for me, pointed a finger in my chest, glared into my Bambi-like eyes.

"You're up first. Don't *bleep* it up," he said. (I was starting to sense a trend.) Then he walked away. *Wait, what?* I immediately broke into a cold sweat. And not a little sweat. I was dripping like a boxer in the ninth round of a heavyweight title fight. *I'm going to throw up,* I thought as I walked into the hall, heading straight to the bathroom to splash some water on my face and try to calm my nerves.

Finally, I stepped up to the podium and looked out over the group of billionaires, NBA brass, and lots and lots of lawyers all staring up at me—or at least I thought they were. As I reflect back years later and have now observed this room from a different seat, most attendees are not interested at all and are on their phones or chatting to the person in the seat next to them. But that was not how I saw it from the podium. Still sweating, I looked down at my paper and read my prepared talk word for word for the next 15 minutes, something that rarely sounds good or holds any interest. (You know when you actually *know* that you were horrible? Yup, that was me.) I was given a platform for 15–20 minutes with some of the most important people in the world of business and sports and I wasted it. No emotion, nothing to drive change, it was just a monotone, get-this-over-with speech. Mark Cuban asked me a question, but before I could formulate a response, David jumped in to answer it. As hard as David was on those of us who worked for him, he wouldn't let anyone else mess with you. He was like a tough yet protective dad.

Brutal, I thought as I shuffled over to my seat. Yes,

I got some token "nice job" pats on the back, but I knew I had done exactly what David Stern told me not to. *I can never do that again,* I thought. And I haven't. What an incredible lesson for me.

★ Grounding Principle ★

I know a lot of people who have the same fear of public speaking that I once had. It isn't comfortable and it isn't natural, but for some of us, it is essential in our role as leaders. After a lot of trial and error, I settled on these four elements to drive the preparation for an excellent speech you are giving or lesson you are teaching: (1) commit to preparation and practice, (2) solicit direct feedback and be willing to receive it, (3) display confidence, and (4) be a storyteller. The four elements symbiotically feed off each other. If you saw me in front of a group today, you would notice that a comfortable presence, a soft smile, and self-deprecating story or two have replaced the sweat on my brow and red face of stress. This only comes after giving thousands of speeches. You might also notice that I have jettisoned my notes and replaced them with a commitment to drive three core messages with accompanying stories; I now have a structure of: tell them what you are going to tell them, tell them, and tell them what you told them. *I have developed this practice that works for me because I failed so publicly.* But instead of curling up in a ball in the corner, I used it as a springboard to get better and as an impetus to help train over one hundred of my coworkers so they too can thrive in front of a group and avoid the fall I took.

Ego Is the Great Deal Killer

After the tough-love truth delivered by Jeff Robinson as detailed above, I eventually found my stride by building relationships, which allowed me to evolve into an executive who walks into situations without preconceived notions or ego. This approach has allowed me to learn and continue to grow while avoiding the death-trap pitfalls in a career on the rise. The story of my dad's professional life is also a good example of this, but unfortunately it does not have a happy ending.

My dad grew up as the fifth of six kids in a two-bedroom apartment in a decidedly lower-middle-class Irish enclave in Bayside, Queens. He would tell us stories about my grandfather, Louis, who emigrated from Scotland, coming to America to play soccer and find work as a package deal. He worked for Metropolitan Life, an insurance company, and was unhappy with his professional lot. As family accounts proudly have it, he was called to testify against his company in a patent infringement case. He told the truth in court under oath, and while the company could not fire him, his professional momentum ground to a halt. He never left the company, as job mobility was limited at that time, but he had traded in any career advancement to retain his integrity. The moral of the story in our house was that we would commit to do the right thing, say the right thing, and make the right decisions no matter the consequence.

My grandfather believed in my dad and spoke to him often about dreaming big. My dad would tell us about his father walking him through the nicer neighborhoods in Queens to show him what was possible. He would later appreciate what his father was doing but, at the time, my father found those walks agonizing, because they were only a reminder of what he didn't have. "Hard work," my grandfather would say. "There is no substitute." Nothing was too big, no dream too high; these were the types of things my dad passed on to me. My dad would always say, "You can accomplish anything you put your mind to, Scott," and, "Do not put a ceiling on what you can achieve by setting the bar too low," and, "Scott, that is ordinary behavior and you have the opportunity to be extraordinary. It is up to you to decide." Although his dad was telling him he could achieve anything, my father was not hearing that message. According to my dad, his sixth-grade math teacher had told him that if his brain were any smaller, it would roll out his ear. *This* drove my father to work harder. He also knew he had to get out of Bayside, so he took one of the few paths available to him at the time to get to college and joined the Marist Brothers, a religious order that allowed young men to serve the church while getting an education.

It took my dad a while to find his professional footing. He started working in administration at the College of the Holy Cross in Worcester, Massachusetts, the town where my older brother Sean and I were born. My father was eventually accepted to a PhD program at the University of Akron. At this time, my brother Michael Jr. was born. My dad earned his doctoral degree and then took a position as dean of students at Mount Saint Mary College in Newburgh, New York, the town where my brother Matthew and sister Shannon were born. Five kids under the age of seven was, I imagine, quite an adventure for young parents. Growing up, we didn't have many material things, and we had even less money. There were days when we had puffed rice for breakfast and lunch and pancakes and peanut butter and jelly sandwiches for dinner. (I remember having cold cuts for dinner one night when I was 12 years old and thinking, *This is incredible!*) Our clothes were all hand-me-downs, and my mom cut our hair herself, lining us up on five chairs in a row and literally going down the line and cutting. In just a few minutes, she would complete five haircuts. I shared a room with my three brothers in our small house and have distinct memories of jumping from one bunk bed to the other and back.

I grew up in a house full of energy, love, and hugs. My dad believed in the science of hugs well before there was actual science. "Seven hugs," he would say. "Get them in, and if you haven't, come on over here and let's fix that now." When I was around six years old, my dad "left" his job at Mount Saint Mary. (He said he left, but looking back we think he may have been fired.) He started his own counseling practice out of our house, helping people deal with personal issues much like a family therapist does today. He then fell somewhat haphazardly into team building. His first contract was teaching the local Newburgh police department to work together more effectively. Each of the first three years he made $13,000, which was not a lot of money even back then, and especially with five kids. That's when my mom started her daycare center, Circle Time, out of the basement of our small house. She was already watching her five young kids, why not watch other people's too? Eventually, my mother would end up buying two buildings and opening schools, one for children in daycare through third grade called the O'Neil School, and the other for special-needs children called the O'Neil Learning Center.

People were drawn to my dad. I remember a lot of people saying he had "charisma," although I had no idea what that meant as a young boy growing up around him. He was very competitive, had a great sense of humor, loved the spotlight, and didn't lack confidence. He used all these skills to eventually sell massive leadership-development training contracts, which took him around the world to clients like Xerox, Mc-Donald's, Texaco, and ADP. However, the best deal he ever did, other than marrying my mother, was convincing her to sell her schools and partner with him.

"Your mother is *the* star," he would say proudly, at that point with a company of over 30 trainers and facilitators. My parents basically taught "life lessons" to sales managers and executives so they could develop their sales teams to achieve better success. (My dad would have liked this book.) The results were astounding. People at those companies saw my father as an interpersonal guru and couldn't get enough of him. He had achieved rock-star status at those companies, and for the first time in his life he was experiencing financial success. Even today, many years later, when I run into people my parents trained, each one seems to have a special memory or recounts lessons learned, evidence of my parents' long-lasting impact.

As a result, our family went from famine to feast when I was a teenager (only to return to famine once again, but we will get to that shortly). We went from a young family on public assistance to one that could afford a house with a pool and where my four siblings and I each had our own rooms. We joined a tennis and golf club in town called Powelton Club, and my mom traded in her old station wagon for a white Mercedes. For the first time in my life, I became aware of material things.

My dad often talked about "mailbox money," which is a business that works for you while you are sleeping. He said, "I'm hand to mouth, and everything I make I have to work for every day. If I get sick or take a vacation, we do not make money. I want a business where it's happening without me." (I wish he had known more about the financial markets and investing, but he knew as little as his teenage sons did at that point.) His entrepreneurial genes took on new life, and he started a few other businesses. One was a database for medical services that didn't go well. A second was continuing education for real estate professionals, brokers, accountants, and doctors, who all needed certification. This was before the internet, so you actually had to go to a location to receive training and pass a facilitated test in order to stay certified in the field. My dad hired my fifth-grade teacher's husband, John, to be president. The company, RETC, got big pretty quickly, and eventually it comprised the largest set of real estate schools in New York, New Jersey, and Connecticut. If you know about growth companies, you know that you are investing in the business well ahead of revenue and profits. Every penny you generate from the business gets funneled back into opening up new locations, hiring new trainers, and marketing. So my dad was plowing every dollar we had, all the money from his training business—which was on cruise control—into securing loans to continue feeding the growth of the business.

Three years into RETC, John proposed that he become an equity partner in the company. By now the company had moved into accounting and other lines of training and had a few sites that were standalone profitable. My dad felt like John deserved equity and upside given the work and progress, and they agreed to structure a deal. That was until John asked for 50 percent of the business. My dad offered him ten. (Today, given my experience, I recognize that 5 percent would be the high end of appropriate.) John said no. They tried to negotiate as my dad explained the investment in the business and necessary cash needed to sustain growth. But they were both overly focused on being "right" and too far apart to find a solution. They were definitely not seeing eye to eye.

The next week, John took the top four executives, all the records, and the database and left to form a competing company in the exact same markets. My dad felt so betrayed and devastated that he became maniacally competitive with John. Before, he was typically hopeful and optimistic; now his sole focus was on destroying his former friend. Because of his tunnel vision, he all but abandoned his core training business, the O'Neil Group, which was funding the cash needs of a growing company. This was a death sentence in the consulting business, where you have to manage the relationships, the flow of information, and how things are going. But my dad cared more about being "right" by destroying John and winning than about being effective in his own business, and to that he experienced his last "success" as both businesses failed. One night at a family dinner, my parents began to argue as my mom told him he had to stop focusing on John, "or you're going to take us all down with you." He didn't listen.

★ Grounding Principle ★

The walls came tumbling down as my dad's core business died a slow, painful death, until we were in a deep hole of debt from which he never recovered. When the situation unwound in its entirety, we had to move out of the house, and my parents separated after 30 years of marriage. What hurt the most was that Lisa and my daughters never knew the incredible strength of the O'Neil family unit, and worse, they never saw my dad as amazing, smart, and funny—only broke, broken, and lonely up until his death. I attribute the great fall to ego and not being able to see past himself or the revenge he sought. He had a great life that was truly something impressive, and then he didn't. But his experience taught me a few lessons, and even though they are probably not the legacy he wanted to leave his son, they remain invaluable.

First, save and invest your money properly so you're not going to be broke. (Save, save, save is a message I drive home almost to insanity to our children, employees, and players.) *The bigger lesson, though, is that ego is the great deal killer in any relationship: between clients, coworkers, employees, spouses, and children.* Last, it is more important to be effective than right, and my dad chose the latter.

Despite that life lesson from my father, there have been times of high stress when I've also gotten caught in the ego net, and they never ended well. An example is one verbal scuffle I had with basketball Hall of Famer Larry Brown, a well-respected former coach of the 76ers. Larry had successfully coached eight NBA teams, including the Allen Iverson–led Sixers, who made it to the NBA Finals in 2001. But when he went on a morning radio program to claim that he could "fix the Sixers in five minutes" and that "they have no basketball people in the organization," I considered it a slap in the face to the organization, general manager Sam Hinkie, and coach Brett Brown (no relation to Larry). Unwisely, I set out to defend the organization publicly, which led to an uncomfortable and awkward back-and-forth with Larry. In the end, I picked up the phone like I should have in the first place. We had a professional conversation and talked about how we could work together in the future. Stepping back, I can see that my actions were out of character with how I work and how I might advise a friend. Why did I go to that place? How did that happen? There was pressure, of course, and seeing friends, coworkers, and people unfairly criticized added to my sense of injustice.

There was a quixotic sense of right and wrong. But what made me act out and betray common sense and rational thinking? Ego . . . and that is something to keep in check. It doesn't stop there, though, as I have had some uncomfortable back-and-forth exchanges with fans and media members, some of which have become public and others likely will be some day. I have learned the hard way that this is not the way to live.

My World's Most Famous Fall

I was 38 years old when I was named president of Madison Square Garden Sports (MSG) for the New York Knicks and New York Rangers. And despite it being 2008, with the economy in the throes of a financial meltdown, there was no place I would have rather been when I got the job. MSG was this incredible brand with indescribable energy and amazing scope. During my time there, we invested over $1 billion to keep the World's Most Famous Arena the greatest on the planet, and the Knicks and the Rangers, respectively, were in the NBA and NHL playoffs. We were in the spotlight again.

But something was wrong. I had always been happy at work—even during my time as a 22-year-old marketing assistant for the New Jersey Nets, typing memos, taking dictation, getting lunch, and picking up dry cleaning. In that job and those that followed, I woke up every day and couldn't wait to run to work.

That's why I knew something was wrong—very

wrong—when I was struggling mightily to find that same passion every morning. My boss Hank Ratner, the CEO, and I had philosophical differences that just wouldn't go away and occurred with increasing frequency. And now that I'd done much of what I'd been brought there to do—the big sponsorship and suite deals were sold, the ticket prices raised, and the return for the project was in the books—I was no longer essential.

For my part, I wasn't living the way I wanted to live. I wasn't having fun. And it felt like every instinct, management lesson, and leadership principle that I believed was necessary to create a world-class place to work was being shuttered, judged, and attacked. I'd come home from work and Lisa would ask, "Are you okay?" I wasn't. "This isn't you," she would say. She was right, of course, but I was having trouble seeing the sun through all of those clouds.

At that point in my life, the World's Most Famous Arena was the wrong place at the wrong time for me. So after four years on the job, I "left to explore other opportunities." That's code in the sports and entertainment business for "I just got fired." Hank fired me professionally, and I believe if you asked him, he would say I left with equal grace. There was no surprise on my face when he let me know, but there might have been more than a little relief. I then had an engaging conversation with Jim Dolan, the chairman, where I thanked him for the opportunity and he thanked me for the work, and we remain friends to this day. That was it, I thought—but it wasn't.

Because that was a high-profile job, my firing was very public. This made the experience much worse—I couldn't just slink off into the sunset as I had when HoopsTV went under. To me, this was a modern-day version of the public guillotine scenes in old movies. News of my firing was in the *New York Post*, the *Daily News*, and the *New York Times*, and seemingly just about everywhere I turned. The one thing running through my mind was, *This is not exactly what I want my kids or my mom reading about me.*

So there I was, sitting in my home office and staring into my laptop screen as the Google alerts hit my inbox. I was convinced that everyone I knew was reading exactly what I was reading, which was all eight articles about my firing and *then* all the websites, comments, and message boards that spun off the articles. Yes, I went way down that rabbit hole. Most other people in the sports business read 50 articles on a variety of subjects each day, many of which they won't even finish, and one about an executive's firing will barely register. Maybe they raise an eyebrow, but they're done thinking about the story the second they move on to the next one. They probably won't even focus on it unless it impacts them directly. (Oh no, how am I going to get tickets to see the Knicks now?)

Yet, when you're in your own fishbowl you don't

realize that. I read *every single* word printed about me. It's the same thing my daughter goes through when someone posts on Instagram that they had a party and she wasn't invited, or when a girl tags every one of her friends in a post except my daughter. *It doesn't matter,* I might suggest to her. Yet, that's the center of her world at that moment, just like I was the center of my own when I got fired. To say I was not in a great mental state is an understatement. Adding to that dynamic were the people close to me and others whom I know and work with who were all reacting in different ways, trying to figure out if they should call, text, or email (the answer is yes, by the way) and, if so, what they should say (the answer is that you should always be authentic and tell the person you love them). So, a lot of interactions became awkward and then I started overthinking everything.

★ Grounding Principle ★

Years ago, my mother shared this great article called "Rewind Your Clock" by Dr. John Gardner, professor of public service in the Graduate School of Business at Stanford University. The gist was that most people are neither for you nor against you, but generally more concerned and focused on themselves. The author goes on to explain that at first this realization is troubling, but as you grow, have more life experiences, and gain perspective, it's actually quite liberating. It took me months to *stop blaming others, focus internally, recover, and be mentally healthy enough to appreciate the incredible people* I worked with, the amazing experiences gained, the friendships, and to be able to smile at all we had accomplished in those four years. As Peter Guber suggested, I decompressed by traveling with my family. I also took stock of my life, reconnected with those in my personal and professional life, and engaged with some friends on projects to keep me intellectually challenged. Importantly, I wrote a filter to guide the next chapter of my career—which included working with people I love, like, and respect, turnaround, a big city on a coast, financial upside, and being a CEO—and then went off to find a new adventure, which I did in helping build HBSE into the sports and entertainment company it is today.

Failing Forward Through Football

Al Guido is one of the most respected business executives in sports as president of the San Francisco 49ers, a storied NFL franchise, and he is also a partner of ours as CEO of Elevate Sports Ventures. What he told me about his experience with high school football could be seen as a "failure," yet it pushed him forward and transformed his life. To me, that's not a failure at all but should warrant a touchdown dance. Al describes his sophomore year at Washington Township High School as one full of bad decisions and a lack of focus on anything but his high school football team, on which he was a standout. "It was one of the toughest years in my life.

My family was struggling at home, I was working at a local Pizza Hut after school at night to try to contribute," Al explains. "My parents were incredibly hard workers, which, later in life, would lay the foundation for the appreciation of effort and persistence. But as a young man, I fell into quite a bit of trouble—skipping school, missing assignments, watching my grade point average spiral. I made many, many bad choices. I felt lost."

Al missed about 40 school days and had poor grades. As a result, he was ruled ineligible for football his junior year. He was so embarrassed that he didn't want to attend the first game as a spectator. Eventually, his father convinced him to go. "Walking to the field from the parking lot, a range of emotions bounced around my head: mad, sad, happy for my friends, embarrassed, and lonely. Even talking about this *today*, so many years later, brings back a pain I can't truly describe," Al says.

★ Grounding Principle ★

As his teammates ran on the field, Al was stunned to see that player after player, friend after friend, had Al's number written on tape wrapped around their cleats. "I don't remember if we won the game. I don't remember the drive home. I only remember the overwhelming sense of commitment, belonging, and love that my teammates had for me. I'd let them down. I'd let myself down, but they were picking me up when I most needed it. I had a hard-core feeling in my gut that told me it was time to change. It was time to show the grit and perseverance that I had as an undersized football player on the field and leverage that in my daily life," Al says. *"It was time to seize my opportunity and embrace the challenge ahead. It was time for me to start my life.* Of course, not every day was great. I had setbacks, but I made it work. That game, with my dad by my side and my teammates in my heart, started the turnaround in my life and will always remind me to push forward and that to be successful I am going to have to commit every day."

Failure Brings Humility, Learning, and Opportunity (Even the "Greatest of All Time" Fall)

Paul Rabil and I met a few years ago when several of my friends invested in the Premier Lacrosse League he founded and suggested he and I spend some time together. Paul is the best lacrosse player in the world— literally—and he looks the part: tall and handsome, with ripped muscles. He also has an athlete's cool demeanor and a viselike grip of a handshake. To top it off, he's smart, serious, and intellectually curious, traits that drew me to him immediately.

Like many of those who have taken chances, led teams, and made it to the big stage, Paul didn't always have the wind at his back. During the 2014 World Lacrosse Championships, the United States was the consensus "Best Team in the World," and Paul was the team captain, the "Player to Watch," and "Best Player in the Game." Yet, for only the third time in history, the United States failed to win the gold medal. "The entire game felt like a blur. We had low confidence, we couldn't catch a break, and they were capitalizing. Worse, we were the home team, but our crowd had been silenced, and the energy had been sucked out of the stadium. I felt numb when the clock hit zero. All I could think about was the long list of people I had let down—lacrosse players, young and old; parents; staff; and everyone I knew," Paul recalls. "My parents were waiting for me when I walked out of the locker room, and I just fell into their arms and wept." Hmmm. I didn't see *that* one coming. It didn't make sense. It didn't add up. *The* Paul Rabil? Really? I thought he was Superman. But that's the point: we all fall, it happens to everyone. It's just that not everyone is confident enough to share a vulnerable story or strong enough to learn a lesson and grow.

Somewhere between picking up a stick for the first time in his formative years and stepping onto the field for the World Lacrosse Championships, Paul's understanding of self became entirely wrapped up in *what* he did versus *who* he was. As a result, on the day he lost the world title, he began to spiral.

"I fell into a quiet, real depression—one that even the comforting adrenaline rush of an intense workout or interval run could not pull me out of," Paul says.

When I heard Paul's story I couldn't believe it. Yes, we all go through tough times, but Paul is like the Michael Jordan of lacrosse. This guy—with all he had going for him—was struggling? It just shows you that no matter who you are, whether you're the greatest of all time— GOAT—or not, everyone is fragile, and we have to take care of our emotions and ourselves. Understanding where he was and valuing help from others, Paul sought out a sports psychologist, assuming the two would analyze his on-field performance and identify cheats to work around the anxiety that affected his game. And they did. But they covered those issues in a matter of days. "What remained, and when the real work began, was tied to deeper and more complex issues: my interpersonal relationships, my ability to listen, absorb, and learn from the world around me, and my ability to derive true fulfillment from inside rather than the name on the uniform or the box score," Paul explains. Of course, he is definitely not alone. Have you ever been anxious walking into a new school lunchroom for the first time, not knowing where to sit? How about that first day at a new job? What about on a first date? At times, we all struggle with feelings of inadequacy, failure, and not measuring up. Yes, it is refreshing to imagine someone so incredible struggling like the rest of us do, and even more important is his willingness to discuss it.

According to Paul, athletes, especially the lonely-at-the-top athletes (and I would argue most people running companies as well), develop a hard shell. Being at the top comes with pressure, along with the assumption that the best player on the field already has all the answers, will be perfect in his shots and passes, and will score the game-winning goal with no time on the clock—i.e., robotic perfection. Star athletes internalize these demands and often form cold, hard walls and barriers between themselves and their teammates, coaches, and loved ones. Moreover, these self-built fortresses decimate their ability to be vulnerable, which prohibits real learning. Unfortunately, the fear of failure, the obsession to maintain the model of perfection, and the pressure to retain the "Best in the World" label eventually paralyzed Paul completely. "I was scoring eight goals in championship games, crushing professional team records, walking away with more MVP trophies than I could remember—but drowning in the anxiety of potentially losing it all," Paul says. "Finally, the fear got so pervasive that I actually avoided any competition I couldn't absolutely win. Soon I was playing down to the level of my fear—overthinking every play, missing easy goals, treating my teammates roughly, shutting down on my coaches." He needed help and he was strong enough to get it. What to do? His sports psychologist recommended he confront these issues on a ping-pong table. Yes, ping-pong.

"Embrace the fire of competition, seek it out," the sports psychologist told him. "The more you put yourself in competitive situations, the more your body will acclimate to that pressure during a game. It doesn't matter if you win or lose, just get back into the cadence of performing under pressure." Paul began to integrate competition into his day-to-day routine. A game of ping-pong with friends. Race you to the car. How many times can you juggle this soccer ball? Slowly, he added layers and layers of competition to his life, seeking those same game-day nerves and acclimating to those paralyzing shakes. For so long, he'd lived on this high, lonely peak of perfection. "Suddenly, I was having fun. Not only that, I began to unabashedly expose my obvious cracks and flaws to would-be friends, partners, or colleagues, and evaluate their ability to provide honest feedback that might challenge my person, businesses, or game to improve," he says. These days, Paul seeks out trainers and training methods that run contrary to traditional lacrosse training. Often he's left ego-bruised and physically sore, but electrified. He'll spend an hour debating on-field strategy with the best rugby players in the world to absorb a new perspective from a completely different game. Mastering the skill of vulnerability and listening opens us to incredible riches.

"Today, the title of which I am most proud is 'entrepreneur'—the definition of which is light years away from the lacrosse player I was when I was 20 years old, but one that makes that lacrosse player a more mindful team leader, a more coachable athlete, and richer in his life beyond the crease," Paul says. "I understand and embrace the ways I learn best, and I systemize those processes to absorb clearly and efficiently. I consume best audibly, so I began a podcast—*Suiting Up with Paul Rabil*—that allows me to study the world's most impressive industry leaders, recite and question what I learned before them, and listen to and dissect their teachings for others to hear."

★ Grounding Principle ★

Paul got knocked off his horse—or maybe his perch as the GOAT—by a very public failure. He wanted to get back up and was *smart enough to get help, listen, learn, and put a plan into action to regain his sense of self and excellence and fail forward.* The last time you were down, struggling, or in a funk, were you smart enough to reach out to get help and open enough to listen and engage to get yourself back up?

♪ Your Turn to Put This into Practice ♪

Identify the three biggest failures, mistakes, or slipups that are on your mind, what you learned from them, and the positive impact the experiences have had on you.

	LESSON LEARNED	POSITIVE IMPACT
Failure/Mistake/ Slipup #1		
Failure/Mistake/ Slipup #2		
Failure/Mistake/ Slipup #3		

CHAPTER 5

Be the Purple Water Buffalo

Never doubt that a small group of thoughtful,
committed citizens can change the world;
indeed, it's the only thing that ever has.
—Margaret Mead

The eyes of a purple water buffalo seem to stare deep into my soul each time I pull into my garage. Now, how the purple water buffalo got into my garage, that is a longer story.

On day two of my job as president of Madison Square Garden Sports, I decided to have an all-staff meeting with the five-hundred-person sports group. There, I showed a YouTube video called "Battle at Kruger." (By now it's gotten millions of views, and if *you* have not seen it, put this book down for nine minutes and watch it. But then come back and keep reading.)

At the meeting, I quickly introduced myself, thanked everyone for coming, and then turned down the lights. The video starts with a group of tourists observing, narrating, and filming a herd of water buffalo at a watering hole in Kruger Park, in South Africa. As the camera pans wider, a pride of lions can be seen crouching and then attacking the herd, eventually pouncing on the smallest, weakest buffalo, a young calf. A particularly aggressive lion jumps on the calf, and the two tumble into the watering hole as the rest of the buffalo scatter from the impending danger. More lions jump in, biting the little one while simultaneously trying to drag him back onto land so they can settle in for an afternoon snack. Just as it appears that they have the proper leverage to get the baby where they want him, a crocodile emerges seemingly out of nowhere and snaps the water buffalo's leg. A tug of war with the baby ensues, but shortly after, the lions pull him onto the shore and get on top of him, trying to kill him. Meanwhile, the tourists keep up the narration, almost like play-by-play announcers calling a big game, saying things excitedly like, "The lions have won! The lions have won!" The camera pans back and reveals a herd of two hundred water buffalo hesitantly moving toward the lions who are trying to eat the young calf. It appears that their apprehension and fear are trumped by their love and commitment to family, team, and herd. The water buffalo come in force and knock the lions off the baby, who then miraculously gets up off the ground and runs away with the rest of the herd.

"Who do you want to be? The tourist? The lion? The crocodile? Or the water buffalo?" I asked the group rhetorically when the video was over and the lights were back on.

So how about *you*? Do you want to be the tourist? Not me. This is the person who watches life going by and doesn't do anything about it. The tourist sits idly on the sidelines while her manager is doing things she shouldn't be doing. The copy machine is broken, and the tourist just moves on to use the one at the other end of the floor rather than taking any steps to fix the machine. The tourist talks a lot, is good at judging others, but rarely steps in to lend a hand or be part of the solution.

Do you want to be the lion? Not me. The lions prey on the weak. The lion yells at the marketing coordinator about a missed assignment or sneers at the young mother trying to wrangle a car seat and two toddlers onto a plane to get them settled. The lion has a big title but has forgotten where she came from, has lost compassion for people, and would rather roar alone than embark on a journey with a team.

Do you want to be the crocodile? Not me. The croc saw a wounded animal and attacked it when it was down. The croc takes a public shot across the bow to the boss when a neighboring department is struggling to meet its budget. The croc keeps lists of friends who make mistakes so he can leverage that information later.

"This incredible place—the World's Most Famous Arena—is filled with water buffalo," I continued, feeling and feeding momentum and hope. "The water buffalo is about team. When coming to the rescue, there are a few of the water buffalo in front who are nervous and hesitant, not quite sure how it's going to go. But when they are standing shoulder to shoulder moving forward together as a herd, they know at that moment that they can accomplish anything as long as they support each other and move to run off the pride of lions.

"The good news," I added, "is that nobody is going to force you to be anything you aren't comfortable with, so if you have different instincts and enjoy being a tourist, a lion, or a croc, that's okay. You'll be just fine."

I paused and could feel some anxious people sigh a bit of relief before I added, "You just won't work *here*." And, there you have it; it was on. We were on our way to building a world-class team. Later that day, Howard Jacobs, who led the marketing team, and Mike Ondrejko, the sales team, walked into my office with the aforementioned soul-searching giant purple water buffalo photo that now lives in my garage.

"Thank you. I absolutely love this. But purple?" I asked.

"Purple is the color of royalty, and we plan on living up to that billing." *So do I*, I thought to myself. *So do I.*

⋆ Grounding Principle ⋆

This is going to be quite a team, I thought. From that day forward, the water buffalo became a symbol and rallying cry of what we aspired to become at Madison Square Garden (and what I aspire to personally as well). We bought buffalo nickels (which, by the way, cost three bucks each), and if one of our colleagues demonstrated she was an extraordinary teammate, a buffalo nickel would be affixed to a card explaining the act of teamwork, and it would be placed on her desk or, oftentimes, taped to the top of the cubicle. A replica of the card would then be taped outside my office, which shortly thereafter looked like a sea of buffalo wallpaper. I loved it and learned so much about teamwork while working there that even now, over a decade later, when one of our newly minted sales associates asks what it takes to be successful in the sports business, I always answer: work unreasonably hard, be intellectually curious, and *be an extraordinary teammate. Be the purple water buffalo.*

Teamwork Makes the Dream Work

This kind of teamwork can occur beyond the office, no matter how young or old you are. A perfect example is a story my friend Sunny Sanyal, the president and CEO of Varex Imaging Corporation, told me about how he came to America after growing up in Mumbai, India. Sunny and I met at Harvard Business School, and I was quickly drawn to his infectious smile, positive attitude, and willingness to help anyone in need. After learning his story, I found it obvious why everyone roots for him. Sunny had lived on his own in Mumbai since he was 16 years old. After that, he went to a university to study engineering. "I was very, very poor, so it was hard enough to pay the $120-a-year tuition. Yes, that is $120, not $12,000, and certainly not $120,000. So I could never afford textbooks, which could cost upwards of $30 apiece," he explains. (Can you imagine trying to get through college without textbooks? Not exactly a recipe for success for most.) Sunny decided to work with others to find a solution. "I figured out very quickly that if I went to bed at midnight and woke up at 4:00 a.m., I could have access to my friends' textbooks because that's when they were sleeping," says Sunny. (He told me this story years ago, but it really hits me today with one daughter in college and two not that far behind. I can't imagine telling them that we can't afford textbooks and that their only option is to wake up at 4:00 a.m. to study by borrowing their roommates' books. Sunny's will and perseverance are remarkable.) But the teamwork didn't stop there. During his senior year of college, Sunny and three of his friends dreamed about going to graduate school in the United States, but none of them had the means to pay the high price of an American education on their own. Still, this didn't deter them. They were so determined that they made a pact: "If we can find a school where even one of us gets a scholarship, the rest of us will pile on and make it happen," Sunny explains. They worked together to study for their entrance exams and carefully picked and applied to the same schools. As luck would have it, three out of the four friends got full tuition and assistance at Louisiana State University (LSU). "It wasn't the first choice for any of us, and each of us had separately gotten assistance from better schools, so we had a choice to make: Do we stick together at a school that's not our first choice or do we go our separate ways to other schools?"

★ Grounding Principle ★

"We realized that we were much stronger together than alone and that there was real value in sticking together as a team," Sunny says. Just like the water buffalo, they moved together, to the United States, pooling their assistance money. When they divided the money that three of the friends got by four, it meant each person got $255 per month. "Each one of us had a specific responsibility within the group. Mine was to pay the rent, another's job was to make sure there was food on the table, the third guy scheduled our coursework so that we could share books and materials, and so on," Sunny says. "When I'd get my $255 at the beginning of the month and then paid our $250 rent, I had $5 left for the rest of the month. But I didn't worry, because I knew I could count on my friends to take care of the food, study materials, etc. We accomplished a lot more as a team than any of us could do individually. There is strength in numbers." After six months at LSU, the fourth friend actually got a scholarship too. "It taught us such a valuable lesson about doing something together and bringing each other along," Sunny recalls. It is always easier to *say* you are a water buffalo than it is to actually *live* as one. But Sunny and his friends' commitment to *hold the team above self and sacrifice on a tight budget was necessary to achieve not only their individual dreams but also those of the team*. Today, decades later, all four friends are successful in their separate careers, and although they are scattered around the country, they remain incredibly close.

If There Is a Piece of Paper on the Ground, Bend Over and Pick It Up

The purple water buffalo attitude can also be summarized in this expression: if there is a piece of paper on the ground, bend over and pick it up. I mean this both literally and figuratively. If you were walking with me in the concourse of the Prudential Center during a concert or a New Jersey Devils hockey game and there was a straw or candy wrapper on the ground, you'd see me bend over and pick it up. Figuratively, what I mean by this statement is that we have to solve problems when we see them. Don't wait. If something goes south, fix it. Now. At the office, it can be as simple as the water cooler being out of water. You don't actually have to solve the problem and get the large and heavy plastic water bottle yourself. Just be accountable and make sure someone attends to it so your teammates will not encounter and be held back by the same issue you just found. Flag it. A light is out in the bathroom? Don't just walk in and walk out. This also relates to bigger issues. At the 76ers, if we get 15 complaints about a season ticket member event we ran, that is good news, because now in our post-event download, we have data points to detail and fix for the next time. We are not perfect, but we can learn, get better, and address the complaints to improve the next experience. Just address the issues as they come up. Do it yourself or give it to a manager or send me a note, but do not step over that paper on the ground.

My first day as CEO of the 76ers in Philadelphia, I brought the whole senior management team together. (I guess this is a thing with me.) I was succeeding a good friend and outstanding executive, Adam Aron, who is now the CEO of AMC Theatres, the largest movie theater chain in the world. He had come in as part of the ownership group to assess and stabilize the organization, as well as set it up for long-term success—which he did.

"We're going to build the greatest place to work in

the world," I told them. "We are going to be respected for the work we do, and we are going to sell out every game because we're going to put together the greatest experience in the world. To get there, we're going to have to raise our expectations."

I was addressing a senior team at an organization near the bottom of the standings both on and off the court. "Now, there are 3,500 season ticket holders. In three years, we will have 12,000, be among the league leaders in full-season ticket sales, and completely remake our brand. Everyone in the world will understand who we are, what we're about, and, by the way, we're going to grow through acquisition, so we need to get this business humming at a very high level quickly," I added. I imagine some people rolled their eyes because the lofty goals seemed unreasonably high and the team had not even come close to those numbers since the peak Allen Iverson era a decade earlier—when he led the 76ers to the NBA Finals. They were probably thinking, *He doesn't understand these fans. He doesn't understand Philadelphia. This is different. We are different.*

Then I said, "Let's go on a tour of the office. Just bring a pad and pen and write down what you see and experience." This is always a good way for me to see who is asleep and who is awake. Plus, the condition and care of the physical plant, the office environment in which you work, tells as much about the culture there as your home might tell a visitor about you. As Hugh

Weber, president of HBSE, is fond of reminding me, culture is what you tolerate and what you celebrate . . . and the condition of the office often reveals both.

"What did you see?" I asked as we settled back down in the conference room after our 30-minute observation tour.

"There is duct tape on the carpet," one person said.

"There are chips in the wall, and a lot of the photos on the wall could be updated," added another.

"Is that it?" I asked.

"Yeah."

"Are you sure?" I asked. They all nodded.

"There is a Coke machine in the kitchen," I said.

"Yeah, it's been there since we moved in here three years ago," said someone (who isn't working with us anymore).

"But we're a Pepsi team, aren't we?" I asked, knowing Pepsi was one of our larger sponsors, and as they were paying us to be part of the 76ers family, it was appropriate to support them off the court.

"Um, yeah," I heard from someone.

"I want it gone by lunchtime," I said as we broke to continue on with the rest of the day. That was paper on the ground, and I was curious to see who was going to pick it up. When I arrived the next morning, I was surprised to find that the darn Coke machine hadn't moved. I called in the same group from the day before. I wasn't asking anyone to physically move it, I was just asking them to get the ball rolling. To do *something*.

"Maybe I wasn't clear yesterday," I said. (Although I may have used some colorful language too.) "The Coke machine is still in the kitchen."

"Scott, it's a little more complicated than you think to get rid of it," said someone else. "It takes time."

"Here's the deal: if it's not gone today, not all of you will be in this meeting tomorrow." My goal was to raise the bar of expectations.

"Who is going to have this removed?" I asked.

One guy, Larry Meli, now the president of our G League team, raised his hand, and sure enough, the Coke machine was out of there by noon.

★ Grounding Principle ★

You are a jerk, you might have thought as you read the section above. Well . . . maybe I could have used a softer touch. And I have actually been called worse. Turnarounds in these situations are not for the faint of heart. To change a culture you need vision, the right people, and buy-in. I have said the wrong thing more than a few times, raised my voice on occasion, and definitely set unreasonably high goals for the team I lead even when things are calm, smooth, and going according to plan. However, everything had to change if we were inheriting an organization in an incredible sports city like Philadelphia, but among the cellar dwellers in both season ticket sales and sponsorship revenue, with a tired brand and a team that wasn't projected by any basketball experts to set the world on fire. Maybe I could have done it in a nicer way, but in a need-to-change-now environment, you do not have the luxury of time or patience. And, in most of these situations, the executive turnover is very high. In the case of the Sixers, it was no different. Of the 250 Sixers employees today, only about a dozen remain from that original group seven years ago. *It is critical to find out who your water buffalo are, as well as your lions, crocs, and tourists.*

Getting Through a Hurricane Together

So, what about at home? Does it matter? Can you be a water buffalo at home too? I sure hope so. How about doing the dishes or your laundry or simply picking up after yourself? (Wait, I hope my daughters are reading this.) How about in your community? Of course! As you look around, you're going to see a lot of tourists, lions, and crocs, and you have to decide how you are going to spend time on the savanna that is in need of more water buffalo.

My friend Hugh Weber's story is a great example of being a water buffalo. We all know the incredible damage caused by Hurricane Katrina in 2005, but Hugh never thought his marriage would be a casualty.

At the time, I worked at the NBA in the TMBO group directly alongside team executives to help gather and share best practices. Hugh was named president of the New Orleans Hornets (the NBA team now known as the New Orleans Pelicans). Because of the hurricane, the staff scattered across the country, and Hugh's family left their home in New Orleans and were living in Charlotte. When the Hornets were temporarily relocated to Oklahoma City, Hugh went through the steps to reassemble the team, knowing that he, too, needed to follow suit and move west. He and his wife decided to live in separate states during the week and have Hugh come home nearly every weekend. This would prevent yet *another* move for their four children and keep them around extended family. Unfortunately, Hugh's marriage couldn't survive, and by the time they settled back into their house in New Orleans 15 months later, Hugh's wife wanted a divorce. "There was so much built-up resentment and the chasm created was so deep that it was irreparable," Hugh says. They lived in separate houses in New Orleans for three years, sharing custody of their children. Then Hugh got offered the job of president of the New Jersey Devils, a great work opportunity that he just couldn't pass up. Not wanting the kids to be away from their father, Hugh's wife sold her house and moved to New Jersey too.

★ Grounding Principle ★

"When we couldn't find a house for my ex-wife in New Jersey, she moved in with me, and we've been living together raising the two of our children who are still at home for the last seven years and counting. It was a big sacrifice, but our number-one priority was, is, and always will be what is best for the kids. Ultimately, I think she asked herself, 'Are they better off with their dad or not?'" Hugh says. His ex-wife moved her whole life for the team—her children—and both parents put their lives on hold because of their love for and high commitment to them. "Right now, the children may not realize our sacrifices because this is normal for them. But one day they'll see that this was a gift we're giving them," Hugh says.

Wait, what? Hugh is living with his ex-wife in the same house? Yes, you read that right. Yes, that is Hugh. He is the consummate teammate who always sees the forest when others just continue to stare smack dab into the trunk of the first tree. He is wholly rooted in his commitment to his children, and that value-based focus allows him to create an environment like this and make it work. How many divorced couples do you know who would do the same? Not many. But Hugh and his ex-wife clearly *value the "we" over the "me."*

From a Potential Death Sentence
to a Dream

A perfect example of the water buffalo mentality can be seen in the millions of healthcare workers who stepped up during the COVID-19 outbreak in 2020. They didn't know how things would turn out, they didn't know if they were going to get the virus or pass it on to their families—in fact, many didn't have the protective equipment to prevent this and expected that they *would*—and yet they stood together to care for some of the sickest people they'd ever encountered. At a time when the easiest thing to do would be to retreat and run away, at a time when their colleagues were dying too, they came to the rescue together. When New York expressed a serious need for more health professionals, an amazing twenty thousand volunteers—yes, *volunteers*—from other states around the country immediately raised their hands and came to help, expecting nothing in return. There were so many other water buffalo during that outbreak—the volunteers who delivered groceries to people who were homebound and those who got together and helped celebrate one woman's one hundredth birthday by standing on her lawn, six feet apart, with balloons and signs, serenading her. The other water buffalo were the millions of UPS, FedEx, U.S. Postal Service, and Amazon employees who took a risk so that the rest of us could follow the mandate to stay home yet still receive all the important items—like food and medicine—and not-so-important items—like puzzles and crafts projects—that we ordered online. I remember hearing one UPS worker on the news saying that he felt "privileged that we're still able to work and do our job." Yes, he said *privileged* to risk being exposed to a serious and potentially deadly virus. Supermarket employees and those who worked for food delivery companies were also taking one for the team. One truck driver for FreshDirect, the online grocery store, said, "It's crazy to understand how much people need us right now. It's a risk coming outside every day to do your job, but I appreciate it, and I kind of feel like a superhero in a sense." Yup, you could say that.

Other heroes during COVID-19 were some of today's young athletes. You know why? They just *get* it. They get the concept of team and continue to raise the bar in understanding their reach, creating a platform, and making a difference for those who need a lift. Social activism isn't new, but the trend of young athletes using their social media muscle and opening their wallets to make a difference continues to make me smile, and I know the world is a better place with these young men and women stepping up and into their roles as world leaders. Several of them kicked it off with significant announcements. Ben Simmons organized the Philly Pledge, a platform where you could find verified local nonprofit organizations that were helping those less fortunate in the battle against this invisible disease. Many of us sat home *wanting* to help but couldn't because of social distancing, so the Philly Pledge made it easy for so many people to donate to local organizations. These pledges started at just $25, so anyone and everyone could help. Joel Embiid donated $500,000 to help provide more personal protective equipment and started a funding campaign to help frontline workers get crucial COVID-19 antibody testing. Al Horford donated $500,000 to help his home country, the Dominican Republic, and each of the five U.S. regions in which he has played basketball.

My bosses, Josh Harris and David Blitzer, and their partners Michael Rubin, Rodger Krouse, Marc Leder, and Marty Geller, along with the New Jersey Devils and Philadelphia 76ers organizations, also made a huge difference. They committed over $7 million to buying ten thousand computers so students in Philadelphia who didn't have access to them at home could take part in distance learning. They also made major donations to Philabundance, which would help feed 160,000 people in Philly, and Newark's grocery program, which purchases groceries for families in need. Another six-figure donation helped RWJBarnabas Health, a network of healthcare providers in New Jersey, buy scarce yet critically important N95 respirators, surgical masks, gloves, gowns, cleaning supplies, hand sanitizer, eye

protection, and ventilators. Another six-figure dona-
tion helped the Children's Hospital of Philadelphia
provide telemedicine visits for children. And these are
just a few examples, a *fraction* of the things they did.
Our players, our teams, and HBSE leveraged their
platforms to share messages of hope, mobilize our fans
and communities, and support those in need. It is just
more proof that, as a team, our intentions and actions
can make a difference in a time of crisis. One $25 do-
nation may not do much, but hundreds and hundreds
of them do! Although they were isolated during the
quarantine, these water buffalo saw that they could still
give as one team, and I couldn't have been more proud
to know them.

Another health-related story that comes to mind
hits close to home. As I mentioned in chapter 1, my
brother Michael—my closest confidant—was three
years into a four-year JD/MBA program at Georgetown, engaged to an amazing woman, Wendy, and
planning his wedding when what started as lower back
pain became excruciating as it spread around to his
stomach. When he woke up from his emergency upper
endoscopy, he looked to his left and saw his fiancée
sitting in a chair surrounded by bridal magazines, crying. "On the bed tray were four color photographs of
the inside of my stomach that showed a really nasty-
looking tumor about the size of a small orange," he says.

The doctors thought it was stomach cancer, so they'd scheduled him for surgery two days later. "If it works, you'll have a relatively normal life," the doctor told him.

"And if it doesn't?" Michael asked. His voice trailed off, as he was too lost in his own thoughts and fear to hear the answer. As Michael describes it, "That was a very surreal moment for a 28-year-old with the whole world in front of him."

During surgery, the doctors cut out about a third of his stomach. Then he had nine days in the hospital to heal and wait for the pathology to determine if the tumor was malignant or benign. While the care was outstanding, the patient experience was awful. "I spent 14 hours a day wide awake, very anxious, with a lot of acronyms thrown at me and new doctors and nurses coming in and out of my room at all hours," Michael says. "They'd ask the same questions that another doctor or nurse had *just* asked and I had to retell my story over and over and over. Nothing felt coordinated, and it was unsettling and anxiety provoking for me, my fiancée, and my family." Lying there, sick, in pain, frustrated, and scared, Michael thought, *If I survive this, I'm going to spend whatever time and talent I have to make it better for the next person.* The idea hit him to turn the typically unused hospital room TV, with its staticky channels, into a hub for a patient's health information and experience. Although it sounds like an entrepreneur cliché, Michael was literally drawing his plan on a napkin from his break-fast tray.

★ Grounding Principle ★

After the surgery, Michael went through four cycles of chemotherapy and missed the last four months of school. In the fall, he returned for his final year 15 pounds lighter and with a bald head. The cancer was behind him, and he still had to make up missed work from the previous spring while doing the coursework for that year, so at this point who could blame him if he let go of that hospital-bed pledge? Cancer had taken enough from him, so he was justified if he wanted to move on. But being the purple water buffalo that he is, Michael did the opposite. Not only did he embrace what happened, but he also used it as a catalyst to make life better for hospital patients so that no one would have to experience what he did. He leveraged that last year of school to take every class he could that would allow him to work on and research a concept he called "interactive patient care." He did it for the team.

The goal was to use technology to *really* put patients and their families in the middle of the care. "I wanted to educate, empower, and engage them where they are in the driver's seat," Michael explains. "I knew this could have a fundamental and sustaining impact on their experience and the outcome of their care." As part of his entrepreneurial research class, Michael found five hospital CEOs who let him survey their patients, families, and staff. "When I came back and presented the research to their executive teams and explained the concept, two of the five signed three-year contracts to license the software," Michael says. In the end, this became the GetWellNetwork, a virtual patient-care navigator for patients and their families that helps control every day of their hospital stay. When Michael talks about his experience, he calls it the "cancer club." Why? "Because we all have to take care of each other," he says. And he stuck to that even when he was down to his last $1,000 and had to take out a second mortgage on his house. Today, 15 years later, the GetWellNetwork has six hundred provider organizations and ten million patients and families across the world, from the United States to Australia.

And when COVID-19 reared its ugly head, overwhelming those hospital systems, Michael redirected his engineers to create a GetWell Loop for companies, cities, states, or any group to provide an app for patient self-monitoring. There was no cost for the app for a health system or company or state, because while some were drastically bumping up the price of ventilators and face masks, *others were leveraging who they were and what they could do for humanity . . . and those are the buffalo this world is celebrating.*

❧ Your Turn to Put This into Practice ❧

A Different Kind of Four-Square Game

- First, make a list of ten people in your life from work, community, school, and friendships with whom you spend the most time.
- Then, put each person in one of the four boxes below.
- Finally, circle the names of the people in the water buffalo box and spend more time with them.

TOURIST	LION
CROCODILE	WATER BUFFALO

CHAPTER 6

Assume Positive Intent

Whatever anybody says or does,
assume positive intent.
You will be amazed at how your whole
approach to a person or problem
becomes very different.
When you assume negative intent,
you're angry.
—Indra Nooyi

What would happen if you assumed in every interaction—meetings, phone calls, texts, social media posts, and conversations—that the other person was kind, generous, and loving regardless of any past experience you've had with them?

What if you approached each of these interactions as if they were unique events, unencumbered by your mood, insecurities, or the pressure of the moment?

What if you assumed positive intent from those with whom you connect, no matter how many alternative and less generous assumptions were possible?

Life would be better.

Assume positive intent, or API as we call it in my house and at work, is a powerful phrase that reaffirms the commitment we've made to value and treat each other with respect while giving the other person the benefit of the doubt. At the core of API is the belief that most people are good and have the best intentions, generally want what is right, and, until proven wrong, will approach the opportunity open and free of your burdens.

API best prepares us to live a life open to possibility. When I am in the right headspace, I assume positive intent in my interactions with my wife, daughters, friends, colleagues, and partners. Life is different when I "API"; it is brighter, fresher, clearer, and more likely to provide a positive outcome. Why? Because we often have preconceived notions about what other people are thinking and what their intentions are, and typically these preconceived notions are negative. More importantly, they are at best clouded and at worst wrong, and they always impact your ability to be effective.

When your phone rings and you look at the screen and realize it's your boss calling, and you immediately get a rush of anxious energy and frustration in anticipation of what you will hear . . . that lets you know that you are not assuming positive intent.

When you interpret a colleague's short text, "I have some feedback for you" with a groan and an eye roll—that lets you know that you are not assuming positive intent.

When a friend leaves a voicemail saying, "I have to reschedule for tonight," and you assume she got a better offer—that lets you know that you are not assuming positive intent.

When your roommate borrows your shirt for a date and you stare her down as she walks out the door—that lets you know that you are not assuming positive intent.

When a FOMO-induced social media post sends your teenager into a tailspin—that lets you know that your teenager is not assuming positive intent.

When a car changes lanes abruptly, cutting in front of you, and to retaliate you lay on the horn, hard—that lets you know that you are not assuming positive intent.

Quick to jump. Quicker to react. We need more patience. We need to give each other a break. We need to "API." Don't look for land mines. Don't seek out cracks. We all can improve upon this practice and become more diligent and committed to approaching others with optimism, respect, and curiosity. Think about a hard conversation or two that you've had recently and ask yourself: Did I give the other person a chance? Or was I so convinced as to what would happen that my thoughts, defensive posture, and self were wrapped up in that predetermined result? And was the result that you assumed was predetermined actually correct? Instead, what if you API? In other words, what if you approach those conversations with the assumption that they may be moments to learn from? To teach? To inspire? To be inspired? To be empathetic? To share? How much richer would your relationships be if you approached every interaction with your family, friends, colleagues, leaders, and coaches with the assumption that you could both emerge better from the engagement?

API matters at home. The letters "API" are actually carved in a piece of slate that is the last thing my wife, three daughters, and I see leaving our house before we go out into the world. Are we perfect? No. Not even close. But we recognize and discuss when we fall short. We try, we engage, and we get better. We use API as a common language to defuse issues and confrontations and to set the expectation that together we can get better with some compassion and understanding for each other in the moment. Most times, what we are hearing and how we are reacting has more to do with *you*, the recipient, than it does the sender. That interpretation has your mind spinning in a negative direction. *How could she say that to me?* or *Why is he yelling at me?*

A simple yet all-too-real-life example in my home might occur if Lisa says to one of our daughters, "Hey, can you grab the clothes off the stairs on your way up to your room?" If our daughters are not API, they will hear, "Grab your clothes off the stairs, you ungrateful and lazy child." If they are API, they will hear, "Can you please help me out and bring the clothes up to your room so no one trips and falls?" Amazingly, something so simple can be interpreted so differently. When you assume positive intent, you are living differently, hearing more clearly, and experiencing a more positive philosophy of life. The before-school chaos in our house often reveals the power of API, or in our case, what happens when it goes out the window. When my girls are at their worst, it's unbelievable what can ensue when someone accidentally spills some juice or is "caught" borrowing a shirt without asking. API! Please. API! Nobody is purposefully spilling juice. I promise. API. If someone borrows your shirt, maybe she needed a shirt. Maybe she was having a bad morning and struggling with what to wear. Maybe her laundry is a bit backed up. How badly do *you* need that shirt? And do you need it *right now*? API. It's important that we all get better about assuming positive intent at home.

API matters at work just as much. We once had five hundred season ticket holders from the New Jersey Devils mistakenly receive a Philadelphia 76ers marketing message. These teams are not only in two different sports—hockey and basketball—but they are in two different *states*, and let's just say the respective fan bases do not typically find themselves warm and fuzzy with each other. This mistake was made by a young marketing coordinator who had been working around the clock trying to hold it all together while her quality assurance manager was on vacation. This was about to get choppy—internally and externally. Fans were confused, and some were furious. Now, if there was ever a time to *not* assume positive intent or to think, "Are you an idiot? Do you know the risk you just exposed us to?" this was it. This situation was tough in the team business because her mistake put the organization in harm's way with our most loyal fans and exposed us to ridicule in the media. But what good would come of saying or texting language like that to her? None. She would have been disenfranchised, as would her friends at work. Our emphasis would have been focused on the problem rather than the solution. Instead, we assumed positive intent. We delivered the message to her in a way that we would like to have it delivered to us. (Then, of course, we talked about processes and set up new protocols to make sure it doesn't happen again.) But, the *how* matters at work as much as the *what*.

A Prince's Inclination

As I mentioned, part of API is to give each other a break and not be so quick to jump or react. I also mean to not be so quick to judge one another—something especially important today, when we need more equality in the world. An example of this comes from H.H. Prince Bandar bin Mohammed Al-Saud, a good friend I met through my brother Michael. And yes, he is actually a prince and a member of the royal family of Saudi Arabia, and the "H.H." stands for "His Highness," though he is quite humble about it, insisting on being called Bandar by those fortunate enough to meet him. He was born in Washington, DC, raised in Northern Virginia, and attended college in Boston. His mother, a Palestinian whose family was among many in the Palestinian diaspora, and his father, a prince, were part of the ruling family in Saudi Arabia. Growing up Middle Eastern in America, Bandar experienced racism and prejudice. His first memorable encounter occurred when he was in seventh grade. His parents had switched him from a private Islamic school (which taught all the traditional subjects in addition to a couple of Islamic and Arabic classes) to a local public school. Even though he was born and raised in Washington, DC, this was his first experience in a non–Middle Eastern or Muslim-majority classroom. One day during history, the teacher was talking about the Israeli-Palestinian conflict. "Having a Palestinian mother, I knew quite a bit about the conflict. The facts the teacher was sharing with the class were not all correct, but I kept quiet as it was mostly harmless inaccuracies," Bandar explains. But then the teacher referred to a picture in the textbook of a young Palestinian boy who looked like he was around Bandar's age at the time. He was pulling a slingshot back with his hands, targeting something in the distance.

"It's such a shame that these kids aren't raised better

than to act so violently and barbaric," the teacher said. At that point Bandar felt compelled to engage and bring some balance to the conversation. "She was no longer sharing small inaccuracies, but a sentiment of hers that was stated in fact, and I was not comfortable with that," he says. "After all, in another time, in another place, that same young boy could have been me." When Bandar asked the teacher why she said the boy was not raised right and told her that the boy could have been him, the teacher shook her head.

"In the Middle East, unfortunately, they are taught that violence is the answer," she said. "But you were raised here so you were taught better." The young prince was shocked that someone in a position of authority was making such a statement based on such misinformation and a bias she had no idea she was espousing and teaching. "Before that, I'd been in a bubble and didn't understand the lens through which people saw me. That teacher's comment popped that bubble and showed me how people viewed me. Actually, it shattered the lens of how I thought people viewed me," he explains. That moment shaped the young prince, pushing him to wash away preconceived notions, work through bias, and understand the judgment-at-first-sight mentality. Bandar understood how people can wrongly perceive and misjudge each other based on their faith and ethnicity, and he was convinced he could help change that notion. "There's a level of misunderstanding in the world we have to appreciate. We also need to know that we won't always understand everyone, but we must always make room for them even when different. I want to do more to raise awareness and make that gap of misunderstanding smaller," he explains.

As a result, Bandar started a photojournalism project, taking pictures of all different types of people in Saudi Arabia—tall, short, black, brown, white; redheads, brunettes, and blondes; those with blue eyes and those with brown eyes—and sitting and having conversations with them, creating a story of the faces of Saudi Arabians. "I never liked the saying 'put yourself in their shoes.' It's not fair to anyone, it belittles one's life journey on one side, and asks the impossible from the other. But by hearing people's stories and thoughts, we get a glimpse of their lives," says Bandar. "For our portraits, we're actually looking at superficial differences that people tend to avoid. We want to celebrate those differences, only to later dig in deeper and show the viewers our shared insecurities and that even after a list of our differences stop, our similarities keep going for a lot longer." Bandar started this project before the recent public movements about race, because it's always been a topic of discussion for him, like it is with many others. "Today it's more pivotal than ever. As much as we are different, we are even more the same in my country and around the world," he explains. "Let's not make what's on the outside of us speak for what's on the inside."

Bandar's personal experiences with racism, especially the classroom experience from his past that took place at such a young age, gave him an openness to explore our differences. By assuming positive intent, he doesn't judge others by their background but seeks to go deeper, and he's trying to share this through his photojournalism exhibit. The goal of the project is to challenge our bias and invite the world to accept more, love more, and assume positive intent.

Abandon Predetermined Instincts

Another example where an absence of API had a long-lasting negative impact comes from a story of one of our tremendous, inspiring emerging stars at the Philadelphia 76ers named Jill Snodgrass. Jill was born in Korea and adopted by an American family when she was six months old. When she was in seventh grade, she found the folder in her parents' basement with her adoption papers and information. The first thing she saw when she opened it was the word "abandoned" stamped in red across one of the pages next to "status of child." This was simply too much for a 13-year-old girl to process. Immediately, she closed the folder and burst into tears. "I'm worthless. I've been abandoned," she thought. She didn't tell anybody about what she had seen. But she couldn't seem to shake the idea of being left on the side of the road, which is the image that the word "abandoned" conjured up for her—even though that's not at all what happened. Jill explains further, "The more I shut down, the higher I built my walls. Relationships were hard after that, and trusting people was even harder."

Twenty years later, Jill was asked to facilitate a session at our company's annual Go Forward leadership conference, which is one of my favorite experiences each year. While it is considered a tremendous honor to be asked to lead a session there, it requires hours of preparation and work, tough feedback from your peers during training, and pressure to share a vulnerable experience from your past. Historically, the facilitators have opened their sessions with teaching stories to tee up the topic, but few, if any, were as unforgettable as Jill's. "I knew I wanted to dig deep too, I just wasn't sure where to dig or even where to look for a shovel. Then I remembered the folder," Jill says. She flew back to her adopted parents' home that weekend and immediately headed for the basement to unearth the packet. She shuddered as she opened it, but this time she read past the first line. There in the notes, past the dreaded stamp of "abandoned," Jill learned that her birth mother only had a second-grade education and cleaned houses to make ends meet; her birth father only had a fifth-grade education. They had moved in together when Jill's mother was pregnant, but her father left shortly before she was born. "I stopped for a few minutes and thought about my mom and how she must have felt. She was poor and alone with a baby that she couldn't afford, a baby she couldn't give a good life to. I sat and cried, feeling sad, ashamed, and an overwhelming sense of love for her and for my mother who raised me. For the first time, I could process the word 'abandoned' as just a legal term and realized that it didn't, couldn't, or shouldn't define me; in fact, it did not even describe what happened. I wasn't abandoned; I was actually saved," she says.

All those years, all that resentment, frustration, distrust, and bad feeling came to a screeching halt. Jill was finally ready to assume positive intent, and, as a result, her perspective shifted, from the shame and anger of being abandoned to recognizing that her birth mother made the ultimate sacrifice so Jill could live a better life. "I thought about that uneducated woman pregnant, alone, and cleaning homes to make ends meet. I not only felt compassion for her but also an overwhelming sense of gratitude and joy for how I was raised by my incredible adopted parents in America," Jill says.

★ Grounding Principle ★

As I sat in the audience fighting off tears, I paused for a minute and looked around. Clearly, I was not alone in being overcome with emotion from Jill's story. As I continued to scan the group, I wondered how many of us could heal a relationship or mend a part of ourselves—even a part of ourselves hurt long ago—by simply assuming positive intent. A month later I followed up with Jill to see how she was doing. She said *the experience was transformational. It changed the way she felt about herself and helped evolve her work and personal relationships.* "More than anything, thinking I was abandoned kept walls up, and if you have walls up you don't let people in all the way," Jill explains. "As a result, I deprived myself of human connectivity and deep relationships and how they mold and shape you." Once those walls came down, Jill was able to open up and trust other people for the first time. She started dating again and even found herself being a more effective and compassionate leader with her team at work.

Act As If

Merrilee Boyack was a freshman at Brigham Young University when her life was profoundly changed in a matter of minutes. She was on campus a week early for orientation and was lonely and very homesick, which she describes as "the terrible, physically, full-on, ugly-crying homesick." Feeling miserable, she dragged herself to one of the orientation meetings taking place in the student center. Sitting in the far corner, upset that she didn't know anyone, and feeling confident that she wouldn't meet any new friends, she saw a professor with a microphone call two young men from the au-

dience up to the stage. The professor whispered something in the first young man's ear. That young man then
walked across the stage with a big smile, waving and
pointing to people in the audience. Then the professor
whispered something to the second young man, who
shuffled slowly across the stage, hanging his head and
staring at the ground, never looking up at the people
in the audience. The contrast between the two men
was glaring.

"Which of these young men would you want to meet
and talk to?" the professor asked the audience.

"The first one," everyone called out at once.

"We wouldn't want to interrupt the second guy's
pity party!" someone shouted.

"The first guy was super friendly!" added someone
else.

"Which of these young men is acting with his true
personality?" the professor asked.

The audience members who so confidently yelled
out answers to his first question seemed stumped as
they sat thinking, *How could we know the answer to that
question? They are both total strangers.*

"You had no clue who was truly friendly or truly
shy. You were just responding to how they acted," the
professor explained. "This is called the 'Act As If'
principle. If you act a certain way, people will interact
with you as if that is who you really are. Eventually that

way of being will become more comfortable to you and will shape who you become."

Merrilee sat there in amazement, having learned a life-changing lesson. "That day I felt as if a light from Heaven was shining down! I understood, finally, how to change. I walked out of that class smiling and waving to people across the campus—pretending as if I was an outgoing, confident young woman, even though I was anything but that," she explains. "Everyone waved and smiled back at me. In three days, I kid you not, I had a marriage proposal. No, I obviously didn't marry the guy, but that experience reinforced for me the power of acting as if. In minutes, I was taught a principle that changed everything for me, one simple lesson that has profoundly impacted every single aspect of my life. Decades later, I *still* use it."

★ Grounding Principle ★

Merrilee's story resonates because there have been moments in all of our lives when we have felt weak, anxious, unprepared, and incapable. Her story also incorporates listening, learning, and a willingness to adapt. In her case, it was through adjusting her lens. The lens with which we see the world is so important, and she found the dials fully in her control. *Assuming positive intent is a conscious decision*, as was Merrilee's to "act as if," *and changing that lens will positively impact you and those in your sphere.*

Gratitude

Something else that helps me assume positive intent is practicing gratitude. Gratitude helps you shift your perspective and focus on what you have right *now* in the moment and not on what doesn't really matter in the scheme of life. Those who feel grateful and express appreciation are happier. At home, our daughters keep gratitude journals. This is a book (or notes on your phone or a gratitude app) where you record things you are grateful for in your life. My most disciplined gratitude zealot is our youngest, Eliza, who writes down 12 things she is thankful for each night before she goes to bed. This routine, which was started upon the suggestion of a Sunday school teacher, has been going on for well over two years and counting, and she has yet to repeat an entry. She ends her bedtime routine with a positive thoughts clicker, a click for every positive thought in her head. (It sounds crazy, but if you walk past her bedroom at night you hear click, click, click, click, click, and it makes me smile.) At work, we begin our executive weekly meetings with handwritten notes to someone in our lives we appreciate. With the group of teenage young men I mentor at church, I have them start each session with a text to mom telling her how much she is loved and one thing she does that is really appreciated.

Two years ago, writer and speaker Randal Wright, a friend and mentor, challenged me to rise every morning at 5:30 a.m. for two weeks and meditate before making an entry in a gratitude journal. Randal believes that early morning is the best time of day to set yourself on course. You can be entirely where your feet are with very few distractions and establish a routine that will bring you a grounding peace that will carry forward in your life. Every morning. No excuses.

"Even the mornings I arrive home from an event at 1:00 a.m.?" I asked.

"Yes, especially those days," he responded. (Ha!) My first week of this exercise included the NBA Draft, the NHL Draft, and the NBA Awards Show in New York City. Oh boy, really late nights and early rise-with-the-sun mornings.

Initially I struggled mightily, and I even sent a note to Randal on day two that opened, "Early to bed, early to rise, makes a man exhausted, miserable, and short on patience," tweaking Ben Franklin's words slightly. Maybe it was just the early to bed part I was missing? I'll admit—my initial journal entries following the exercise were less than poetic and complimentary to my good friend. My first gratitude entry read like a list of tardy thank-you notes and a long list of family members: "Lisa, Alexa, Kira, Eliza, Mom, Dad, Sean, Michael, Wendy, Matt, Stacy, Shannon, Jason, Stephanie, Kim, Steve, Ashley, Teag, Jake, Emily . . ." The next two days were a slightly varied repetition of nephews, nieces, cousins, friends from work, et cetera. On the fourth and fifth day, I mused over coaching basketball and mentors who have helped me on my journey. I had finally begun to explore the gratitude space. A week later, things like "clean water," "the peace and quiet of the early morning," and "hearing the birds chirp as the sun rises over the hills" filled the pages. By the tenth day, my skepticism was replaced by a calm, methodic stillness, somewhere between peaceful sleep and what is known as an athlete's "endorphin high."

★ Grounding Principle ★

Eventually, what began as a guilt-ridden chore became the most precious and anticipated ten minutes of my day. I longed for the tranquility and reward of the quiet that is otherwise absent from my typical routine. I started every morning with clarity, optimism, and quiet strength. I was able to tackle the hormonal tornado that is living with teenage girls. (That alone is a reason to meditate!) I was able to tackle my over-scheduled calendar and minute-to-minute calls and meetings, providing more precise direction to my executives. I could tackle the late-night West Coast conference calls because, in seven hours, I had ten minutes waiting for me that was entirely mine. And *those ten minutes would make me a better father, leader, and follower.* Mine has always been a life of action, energy, chaos, and love, and it now included a calm and appreciation I never thought possible.

Can Law Enforcement and API Coexist?

Camden is a proud, old American city in New Jersey, but by the start of twenty-first century, it had become a grim place to live for many people: the poorest city in America, home to almost two hundred open-air drug markets operated with impunity 24/7, with a murder rate higher than many third-world nations. Sadly, Camden had truly earned its distinction as the Most Dangerous City in America.

I know quite a bit about Camden, as most days I go to work there. Thanks to an aggressive tax credit incentive program, the Philadelphia 76ers built their training complex there, just across the river from Philadelphia. This incredible complex houses the most state-of-the-art basketball practice facility in the world. As we were exploring sites, I toured them with the locally revered police chief, Scott Thomson, who served Camden for 25 years. At the outset, it was clear that he was an incredible leader, well respected and loved in both the police department and in the community. He is credited with the incredible turnaround in the city, and he did it by assuming positive intent, a unique approach that was discussed a lot during the protests of May 2020. But everything wasn't always this good for the chief.

On May 1, 2013, Camden authorities officially declared that they had had enough failure. That's the day they abolished their city police department and created a new organization, a county police force dedicated to "Service Before Self," a new vision rooted in community policing, and put Chief Thomson and his progressive philosophy in place. The strategy was to tackle 40 years of intractable societal ills with a different approach. Instead of warriors who had been relying—mostly unsuccessfully—on force and arrests to combat crime, county police officers would henceforth become "guardians" who would build relationships and help to empower Camden's citizenry to reclaim their own neighborhoods. Instead of patrolling in cars with windows rolled up and interacting with the public only during moments of enforcement or crisis, cops would walk the beat and make meaningful human contact to build trust. Assuming positive intent would be the transformational strategy.

The initial departmental response could best be described as one of skepticism. Most cops viewed this identity shift as an invalidation of their years and years of dedicated service. This is a paradox that exists in many organizations: people don't like the way things are, but they detest change. However, residents started to reclaim public spaces, to sit on their front steps chatting with their neighbors, and to once again allow their children to play in front of their homes and ride their bikes around the block—even in the most challenged of neighborhoods—creating momentum. Slowly over time, many of the skeptical cops started to understand Chief Thomson's notion that they could never arrest their way out of the problems facing their city and that this different approach might just work. When they assumed positive intent in the neighborhoods they patrolled, they found their jobs became much easier and more enjoyable. In fact, API begat API. As the residents began to trust the police and assumed positive intent, they began to feel comfortable sharing information with the police. "They started telling us who the really bad people were in their communities, what cars they drove, and even where they hid their guns," Chief Thomson explains. "With this information and support, the police department suddenly had thousands of additional eyes and ears in the community around the clock to help us achieve our mission. But without constant positive human contact, this never would have occurred."

Several months into this transformation, the new vision and ability to API got tested to its core. During one summer weekend, a drug gang conducted three consecutive shootings, trying to reestablish their vise grip on one neighborhood. The residents fearfully retreated back into their homes, abandoning the public spaces that they had only recently begun to repopulate. Streets that were starting to hear the laughter of playing children once again went eerily quiet. The negative element started to lurk in the alleyways, creeping back out into the neighborhood.

"Just weeks before, we had been celebrating the progress made toward building a safer community and enjoying burgeoning relationships. Now, we feared that the ground gained was quickly slipping away and we urgently needed to develop a new tactic," says Chief Thomson, who summoned an emergency meeting of his executive team early on a Sunday morning. The goal was to walk through their vision for Camden, review what had occurred, and formulate an immediate response to quell the spate of violence. With the combined experience of over one hundred years of policing, they began to formulate a familiar battle plan: deploy specialized units, set up checkpoints, flood the neighborhood with officers to make arrests, and issue tickets until the temperature of those streets cooled.

The trouble was that they knew this traditional approach was not enough to curb the violence and sustain any gains over the long term. If it didn't work before, why would it suddenly work now? "At that point, I challenged conventional wisdom with a series of inquiries and propositions juxtaposing what we knew from our years as law enforcement officers with what we had experienced over the last several months," Chief Thomson says. "With that realization in hand, we immediately slammed on the brakes and reversed course.

Orders were given: Cancel the heavily armed tactical teams! Call off the narcotics sweep squads! Place the recalled overtime officers on standby! We decided to try something different, something that would encourage community members to leave the safety of their homes and join us in taking back their streets, something never tried before in policing."

It was the middle of the summer, and children and their families had been cooped up in their houses for days, fearful of the violence. With outside temperatures reaching 90-plus degrees Fahrenheit and a lack of air conditioning in most residences, Chief Thomson and his team thought about what makes kids beg their parents to venture outdoors: *ice cream*! The police department withdrew $5,000 from their asset forfeiture account—cash seized from criminals, mostly the drug gangs that they were hoping to put out of business. They then located two Mister Softee ice cream trucks and stationed them on the two corners of turf that the drug gangs were battling for. With the ice cream trucks' distinctive and welcoming music playing nonstop, children and parents began to peek out of their windows with curiosity. Once the cops on the beat invited a couple of families to join them for free ice cream it didn't take long for the streets to be flooded once again. Camden County officers were taking dessert orders and handing out soft-serve ice cream cones, connecting with the kids and people in the neighborhood unlike ever before. "The result was an immediate return to the streets by the good people of the community, and we were back to the desirable 'tipping point' wherein crime was better suppressed and there were more good than bad people on the streets," Chief Thomson says. "That summer was our 'eureka' moment, and years and years later it still served as our touchstone for how the Camden County Police Department innovates and solves problems." The officers continued to develop relationships with the community and transformed the old "us against them" mentality with other events such as movie nights and basketball games.

★ Grounding Principle ★

The heading for this section is "Can Law Enforcement and API Coexist?" But as Chief Thomson discovered, API combined with law enforcement is a *must* to help keep people safe and improve their well-being. "The way to fix communities is not to have them be afraid of you, but to empower them," he said recently at a ceremony where the Camden County Police Department named one of their administrative buildings in his honor. Years later, Camden is still a better place for the decisions that Thomson made. Crime remains down. Graduation rates are still climbing. For many Camden residents, hope has replaced deep despair, and *assuming positive intent remains the reason the city continues its rebirth.* After the murder of George Floyd in Minneapolis in May 2020, a march was scheduled in Camden to remember and honor him. Who showed up? The police, carrying their own "Standing in Solidarity" banners and walking arm in arm with members of the Camden community. This was under current police chief Joseph Wysocki, showing that Thomson had truly created a legacy.

Everyone Is Having a Tough Day

John Dalton Elton, known as Dalt, was always teaching life lessons to his children. But he didn't just talk the talk; he walked the walk and practiced what he preached, making sure his children learned by example. This left a huge impression on his son, Chester Elton, who is now a bestselling author and motivational speaker. "To me, my dad was almost supernatural; he seemed to be good at everything—a great athlete, a booming bass voice, and a gifted orator—and he was always optimistic and cheerful. He was loved by everyone and kind to every person he met. There was no one I wanted to emulate more or whose approval I sought more than my dad," Chester says.

Dalt had created many family traditions with his wife and children, and one was to shop for bargains. "If you have to pay retail, you just don't have enough friends!" Dalt would say. One beautiful Saturday afternoon when Chester was 12 years old, he and his father headed over to Gastown, a neighborhood in their hometown of Vancouver, British Columbia, on one of their bargain hunts. As they passed Pigeon Park, a place where many homeless people hung out, they saw an older homeless woman cross the street toward them. She was carrying a paper bag stuffed to the brim with her belongings, and as she approached the corner, the paper bag split open, its contents spilling all over the sidewalk. To an onlooker, the items appeared to be of no value, but it was likely everything the woman owned and she seemed frustrated and concerned that all her worldly belongings were strewn in all directions. "I gave the lady a wide berth, broke eye contact, and kept walking quickly away from her toward the other side of the street," Chester says. And he wasn't the only one running away; every other pedestrian in the vicinity followed suit. Everyone, that is, except Dalt. "My dad walked away from me, knelt down to face the homeless woman, and proceeded to assist her in gathering her belongings one at a time," Chester says. "He talked to her kindly and gently. He even said something that made her laugh, and then he walked her safely into the park."

★ Grounding Principle ★

"Dad, you shouldn't touch those people. It isn't safe," Chester told his father afterward. But Dalt shook his head with a look of disappointment on his face.

"Ches, you have to be good to *everyone*. You don't know what they're going through. Everybody is having a tough day," his father replied as Chester felt the heat rising in his face.

"I was ashamed and embarrassed for my reaction, and I felt a renewed compassion for the homeless woman," Chester says. "I also felt pride, love, and respect for my father, and in that moment, I learned the lesson of a lifetime." This is a lesson Chester still recalls, decades later.

"I have never forgotten that moment. It changed the way I look at people. It was the secret to my dad's wonderful way of life. He treated everyone with respect, from the parking attendant to the captains of industry. Everyone mattered to my dad. Everyone was valuable and important in his or her own way. He was kind to them all. If there is one lesson I would hope my children learn from me, it would be to *be kind to everyone—everybody is having a tough day*."

⚘ Your Turn to Put This into Practice ⚘

My father had a navy blue t-shirt that he would wear way too often in the late 1970s and early 1980s. In bold, yellow capital letters it said, "I'M OKAY, YOU'RE OKAY." That t-shirt holds the keys to assuming positive intent. I'm okay: I'm okay with who I am. I am confident and self-assured. You're okay: I am meeting you as you are without judgment or precondition.

Imagine that you are designing a t-shirt to remind yourself and those in your life that you are 100 percent committed to assume positive intent. What would your t-shirt look like?

CHAPTER 7

Trust the Process

*A journey of a thousand miles begins
with a single step.*
—Lao Tzu

On January 5, 2015, 76ers point guard Tony Wroten was interviewed by ESPN writer Pablo Torre in the locker room prior to a game with the Cleveland Cavaliers. "They tell us every game, every day, 'Trust the Process.' Just continue to build," he said.

Trust the Process.

In three simple words, Tony delivered an anthem that is still chanted at games and adorns t-shirts worn by Philadelphia 76ers fans around the world. "Trust the Process" has even supplanted "hello" as a greeting when passing a fellow fan wearing the red, white, and blue. Since half my wardrobe is 76ers gear, Trust the Process has been shouted to me by perfect strangers everywhere from South Philly to London to Shanghai. Trust the Process is so huge that our biggest star adopted "The Process" as his nickname, which is announced before every home game: Joel "The Process" Embiid. But how did we get here? What led to this so-called process, and how and why does it matter on the journey of self-discovery?

At the time, the Philadelphia 76ers were in a rut on and off the court. The once-proud franchise had only won more than 50 games in a regular season twice since 1990. Twice. (A 53-win season in 1989–90 and a 56-win season in 2000–01, when Allen Iverson led the team to the NBA Finals.) The franchise needed a reset, and it got one when the new managing partners Josh Harris and David Blitzer acquired the team and were determined to right the ship through their thesis that patience was the last great arbitrage in sports. In this business, there is too much short-term pressure with media, fans, and even family, so you are pushed to make decisions where speed is valued over lasting impact. However, Josh and David were committed to the latter. Hailing from the world of private equity, these global dealmakers had made their careers buying low, installing new management, providing resources, and focusing on WMI and a long-term view. The Philadelphia 76ers seemed like the perfect jumping-in point in the sports world. This team had all the elements of a turnaround: a large, growing East Coast city with passionate fans, wonderful partners at Comcast, which owns and controls the arena where the team plays, and a league that is expanding and driven. Josh and David were committed to their long-term vision of restoring this franchise to its illustrious roots and were willing to make the changes necessary to get it on the right path.

Okay, back to the Process. Tony popularized the phrase, and the city embraced it: Trust the Process became a movement. When marketing becomes an organic movement, it is a win and an incredible opportunity on which to build. When fans take ownership of the brand and drive it—even pirating t-shirts and selling them on street corners and creating mugs and other items to market on Twitter—you have officially arrived. In the past decade of my journey through the sports business, I have been fortunate enough to be part of two of the most influential movements in team sports history, "Trust the Process" and "Linsanity." The latter occurred in 2011–12, which was my last season with Madison Square Garden and the New York Knicks. Linsanity was the rise of Jeremy Lin, a previously unheralded player who was inserted into the starting lineup. The team immediately went on an epic seven-game win streak, which helped propel the Knicks into the NBA Playoffs for a second consecutive season. Lin's story—an undrafted, American-born player of Chinese descent who graduated from Harvard—caught on like wildfire, and games around the country were mobbed with fans wanting to get a glimpse of this budding su-perstar. Jeremy ended up on the covers of *Time* and

Sports Illustrated and was named ESPN's Breakthrough Athlete of the Year. It was a movement. It was hysteria. It was fun. It was Linsanity. While there are many similarities between the two movements, the biggest difference was the stickiness and length. At the Knicks, we only had a few months to enjoy Linsanity because the Houston Rockets signed Jeremy that summer in free agency after he missed the playoffs with an injury.

The thought process and marketing strategy were similar for both movements: stoke the fire, leverage the team's access to media and the platform, and have the fans own and control it, but do not stake claim, utilize as a marketing slogan, or manipulate around it. Other than some Trust the Process "Hidden Mickeys"—when our designers would hide the letters TTP or "process" in billboards, ads, social media, et cetera, much like Walt Disney has done hiding mouse ears throughout the parks—or an occasional hashtag after a tweet, we held to the playbook for both movements. But Trust the Process was another level, and it wasn't about a player or a person. It is quite possibly the most misunderstood, misquoted, misused, and, in its prime, the most polarizing statement in the history of modern sports.

It all started with the hiring of analytics-driven GM Sam Hinkie. The Process was based on the notion that finishing in the middle of the pack was the quickest way to years of mediocrity. The strategy was to leverage the draft to build a championship-caliber team, and that would take patience. But Trust the Process was never about losing, although basketball traditionalists argued it was, as the worse your record, the better your draft picks. Trust the Process is about taking the long view in decision-making. It is about making a series of small decisions that over time allow for quantum leaps in progress. Trust the Process is about standing strong and making the right decisions without regard for the external pressures that come with running a professional sports team.

And this has as much to do with you and your personal development as it did with the Philadelphia 76ers fans. We need to Trust the Process and have a view longer than the tough moments we find ourselves in, and also have people around rooting for us.

Sports fans around the world following the 76ers during the darkest and toughest years of the Process will acknowledge how hard it was to root for a team posting among the worst records in the league: 19–63 in 2013–14, 18–64 in 2014–15, and 10–72 in 2015–16. Through these years, the team set the longest regular-season losing streak in NBA history, 28 straight games, breaking their own previous record of 26 games set a couple seasons earlier, which they shared with the 2010–11 Cleveland Cavaliers. While some saw this as bleak, pathetic, and distasteful, fan attendance actually grew in each of these three seasons as new fans fell in love with the journeymen players getting a chance, cheered on head coach Brett Brown, and were inspired with the hope that all these high lottery picks would create the superteam of tomorrow.

Fast forward to today, and Trust the Process defines one of the greatest turnaround stories in sports history, as the team was well on its way to a third 50-plus-win season in a row before COVID-19 cut it short. This is more than just a turnaround story. Team president Daryl Morey and GM Elton Brand have brought a vision, stability, and strong culture to the team, now one of the best in the NBA, with a core of young All-Star players like Joel Embiid and Ben Simmons. The team is also leading the league in attendance, and the future looks even brighter as the stars grow into the prime of their careers.

In a world dominated by instant gratification and obsessed by the spotlight of now, Trust the Process is the commitment that you will keep the long-term view at the forefront of your planning and decision-making. This has implications far beyond basketball. Trust the Process is about understanding the mistakes and taking the time to revisit what went wrong and why, and then leveraging that information to get smarter and make better decisions in the future. It takes patience. As Hinkie was fond of saying, "There are no shortcuts to the top, only to the middle." It is not easy, and it can be painful, but in the end Trusting the Process can reap the hugest, most gratifying, and long-lasting rewards.

★ Grounding Principle ★

I have learned many lessons from my experience in and around the transformation of the Philadelphia 76ers from a downtrodden afterthought to a contending team:

Together We Build. This was our marketing slogan in my first season (2013–14) with the team. There are two parts to this: (1) *together we* and (2) *build*. It is better "together," being part of a community. Sports holds a special place in society because it is the modern-day town square. It brings perfect strangers together for a shared purpose. Online or in the arena, we root together, we cheer together, we escape together, we commit together. The "we" matters in life, work, and at home. As for the "build," that is a little more complicated. There is a common belief in the team sports world that you can sell two things: hope and winning. In the absence of both, we sold the "community of we," transparently saying that the process would take time.

Have a Big Vision Even if It Is Ahead of the Market. It is good to be different and see out into the future, to plant your flag in terms of what matters and how you are going to accomplish something. People who do great things think differently, and those who can articulate a North Star provide the best path to achieving something special. Turning around a franchise is a Herculean task, but Josh and David had a big vision to restore the Philadelphia 76ers to its past glory years, a past that boasts such stars as Wilt Chamberlain, Julius

Erving, Charles Barkley, and Allen Iverson—and everyone joining the organization along the way believed in
what we were building toward.

There Are No Shortcuts to the Top. There is no
substitute for the grind, and you need to embrace it.
Do the work. Pay the price. Oftentimes, there are a
million little things that need to get done; your job is
to do them. That is how progress is made over time:
small increments of getting better, and it is just those
things that you can control.

Make Lemonade out of Lemons. We get to decide
what kind of day we have, life we lead, and attitude
we carry. Life isn't ever easy, and the twists and turns
provide opportunities to learn, live, and grow.

Stay the Course. There will be setbacks. You will
have a GM resign through a letter he sends to ESPN
and high draft picks who get injured or don't meet the
lofty expectations. You will say the wrong thing at the
wrong time, your emotions will get the best of you, you
will hire the wrong person and fire the wrong person.
You will trust the institution and rules of the media
and see them abandoned by a wayward reporter; you
will be attacked unmercifully on social media. (I've
blocked over three thousand people on Twitter for
inappropriate language that you wouldn't want your
mother to read.) You will see the true colors of friends
when things go badly . . . it happens (or should I say,
it happened). A team will fall short of expectations,

and some will point fingers and others will run for cover (they did), but we will continue to Trust the Process. High-risk, high-energy change situations are not for the faint of heart. Having a big vision and being all-in comes with risk. Sometimes you will veer off course, other times you will be distracted, and sometimes people might drag you off course. Get back on it. Be patient. Surround yourself with good people who will tell you the truth, and make sure they know you want the truth. Give yourself time and space to think, plan, and reflect on where you are and how to get back . . . but fight through the wind, the rain, and the hail and stay the course. You can do this. You will do this. As I have journeyed through life sharing my learnings with friends, mentors, and teachers, our mutual vulnerability created a common bond.

Clarity of Purpose

A story that really illustrates Trusting the Process was told to me by Rich Gotham, president of the Boston Celtics. Anyone who knows basketball knows that Philadelphia hates Boston. But in the business of sports, it is oftentimes our friends who run the teams that our fans hate. Even your fiercest rivals on the court provide opportunities for you to learn. Rich runs an incredible organization, and it all starts with a unifying, long-term vision that actually says nothing at all.

I was working at the NBA league office when Rich

was named the second president in the history of the Boston Celtics. (The first was Red Auerbach.) I was touring the practice facility, which I try to do when traveling to visit other teams to get a sense of their culture and commitment to development. That's when I looked up at the NBA Championship banners, and there sure were a lot of them. "Part of what makes the Boston Celtics different and such a great institution are the 17 banners that hang in the rafters representing the 17 NBA Championships we have won over the years," Rich explains. "This gives us clarity of purpose: our institution is about winning championships. We take pride in building on that legacy, and it is what motivates us every day to come in to work and get after it." And then he told me the backstory.

In 2008, after winning the NBA Championship, the Celtics were preparing for their summer training camp. Their coach at the time was Doc Rivers. It's funny how things come full circle; today, Doc is the coach of the Sixers and I have the pleasure of working with him and observing his incredible leadership up close. Anyway, back when he was with the Celtics, he had the idea to hang a blank banner in their training complex right next to the 17 NBA championship banners. "We added that blank banner to remind everyone at the Celtics that the journey was not over, we were just getting started, and there was more work to do. We won our seventeenth title and it was incredible, but that was yesterday. We could celebrate the past, but we could not get stuck there, and we needed to turn our attention to winning number 18," Doc says. "The banner was a goal for everyone in the organization to rally around, focus our energy, and commit to accomplishing something special together." From that day forward, anytime Rich or anyone on the team needed a reminder of what they were there to accomplish, they just looked up at that blank banner—their vision for the future. Everyone was working purposefully toward that next championship.

★ Grounding Principle ★

"No, we can't look at the banner every year and realistically say this is a championship year for us. Some years we're rebuilding and others merely in contention," Rich says. "But even when we don't have realistic championship aspirations, what *we're building every day and laying the foundation* for is to fill in that banner."

Have a Big Vision Even if It Is Ahead of the Market

To me, the late David Stern, the legendary former NBA commissioner, was a mentor, a teacher, and the truest example of lifelong learner I will ever know. I am so incredibly fortunate to have had the privilege to work for David for almost eight years, and I am a better leader, husband, father, and friend as a result. Over his 30-year reign, David helped shape and grow the game of basketball into the global phenomenon it is today, while positively impacting so many with his drive, determination, and fearlessness.

When David was hired by the NBA in 1984, he was employee #24—that is, he was the twenty-fourth employee to be hired in the history of the league. To say that the NBA back then was very different from the NBA of today is an understatement. The league office had 20 people, whereas now it boasts over 1,000. The NBA Finals—which today draws ten million households to watch each game in the United States alone—were shown on tape delay. There was no Twitter or YouTube for highlights and not much media coverage. NBA games had half-full arenas instead of today's standing-room-only crowds, and they took place in war memorial fieldhouses instead of in modern entertainment palaces stocked with gourmet food and premium seating.

David's efforts were aided by the Magic Johnson–Larry Bird rivalry, but his global vision for the league was not realized overnight; it did not reap rewards in the short term. Yet as it evolved, it became a force that drove him, and he always Trusted the Process. "In those early days, we had so many challenges both on the court and off. We were scrapping and hustling and trying to pull it all together," David told me. One turning point occurred in 1988, when he learned that Ted Turner, the media mogul who owned the Atlanta Hawks, was going to take his team to the Soviet Union. The NBA negotiated with Turner to make sure that the trip was billed as an "NBA tour," not just one for the Atlanta Hawks. "Mind you, we were not ready or staffed to manage this, let alone optimize the opportunity. But we embraced it and set out to leverage the influence as best we could," David said. When the teams were introduced at the game in Tbilisi, Georgia , in the former USSR, the audience cheered much louder for the Atlanta Hawks than they did for the Soviet National Team they were playing. (Isn't it ironic that the Hawks were playing in a Georgia far from home?) David was shocked. Even more surprising was the endless, thunderous applause for one Hawks player, Spud Webb. David and his NBA colleagues were stunned—and, truthfully, confused—that it was this 5'6" player who was receiving all the attention.

When they asked their hosts why Webb had gotten such an incredible response, they learned that pirated versions of the NBA games that were distributed in Turkey were actually running on television on repeat in Tbilisi, and even being sold on the street. Because it was the year that Webb had won the Slam Dunk Contest, he was a local star. (A little trivia: Webb is the shortest man ever to win an NBA dunking contest, and my guess is that record will stand for the rest of time.) "As I listened to the applause for Spud roar on, I thought, *Yes, there is a market for NBA basketball around the world, and we need to figure this out and start investing*," David explained. He began to craft his global vision for the NBA.

Later, the NBA went to Lithuania to play a game in Vilnius, capital of the country that produces many great players. When David and his wife, Dianne, met the head of the Communist Party there, his first question for David was incredibly telling: Would the Portland Trailblazers' salary-cap situation impact the signing of Lithuanian player Arvydas Sabonis? This was another major sign that there was an international market for the NBA. Taking the long-term view and Trusting the Process, David and his team set their sights on making this a reality.

In the early 1990s, they worked for months and months to get a meeting with the head of CCTV—the largest and most distributed network in China. The goal was to expose basketball and the incredible talent of the NBA players to the largest market in the world. Finally, they were able to schedule a meeting, but when David and his team arrived on the designated date and time, they were told that they didn't have an appointment. Keeping their eye on the prize, David said they would wait in the lobby until the head of the network could see them. And wait they did—for hours and hours. To know David and his level of patience (never very high) and to picture him sitting and waiting for more than four hours in a lobby makes me smile, mostly because I am glad I was not the one who set that meeting up and was sitting with him at the time. It would not have been pleasant. Eventually, the head of the network did come out to meet with the NBA delegation. "We offered to provide them with tapes from our games and said that if they showed them, we would sell sponsorship against them and send them a revenue-share check," David said. "We never sold anything, but we did write them checks." Why? Because David's vision of a global sports league had to include the biggest potential market in the world. Later that year, David sent one of his executives to live in Hong Kong, get a fax machine, and put it in his bedroom. That was their first "office" in China.

★ Grounding Principle ★

"If you have confidence in what you have, what you are doing, and your brand, then just keep pushing, and there is going to be an opportunity," David told me. "We had the Russian deal, we had the Chinese deal, and we had the guy with the fax machine in his bedroom in Hong Kong. Everyone at the NBA was opportunistic, but this international explosion of the league happened because we didn't pretend we knew everything. We kept asking questions, kept reading, kept learning, and kept pushing." Pushing toward a vision. Fast-forward to today: the NBA has three offices in China, and basketball is the most popular sport in the country, with an estimated 300 million people playing. The NBA China business is widely valued at more than $4 billion. CCTV and

Tencent have been incredible media partners in growing the game. After an All-Star NBA career, Yao Ming became an ambassador for the game and continues to be the bridge between the NBA and China. The global vision is realized and continues to this day, as Stern's longtime protégé and trusted advisor Adam Silver is the current commissioner of the NBA. He recently launched a new professional league in Africa with the same global vision, willingness to have a longer-term view, and dedication of resources to drive its success.

There Are No Shortcuts to the Top

The 2013 Wimbledon women's tennis champion Marion Bartoli and I met through a mutual friend who thought I might be able to help Marion with the fashion brand she was launching. I was skeptical of a retired tennis player going into the cutthroat world of fashion. Would she work as hard as she did in tennis to be at the top of the fashion world? (Yes.) Was she talented? (Yes.) Was she smart? (Truth be told, I Googled her before the meeting only to find out she has a genius-level IQ of 175, so, yes.) Marion also had attended a top fashion school in Paris as her playing career wound down and continues to provide television commentary for the four majors (Australian Open, U.S. Open, French Open, and Wimbledon) and other tournaments and still plays in exhibitions. The more she talked, the more I was intrigued by her motivation and the foundation of her iron will and raw work, work, work mentality. I asked what was driving her, and she told me about her childhood.

At the height of the HIV crisis, Marion's father, Walter, was a medical doctor in a small village in France and volunteering at the largest HIV center for Europeans who could not afford treatment. Marion was eight years old when her father took her to the center, where she befriended and connected with several of her father's patients. Just like she did with everyone she met, she told these patients that she was going to be a professional tennis player someday. One of them was Massimo, a 42-year-old new father who took such a liking to this young spitfire that he named his own daughter Marion.

One day Massimo and Marion were talking. "Everything you do, every day, will have an impact on your future. Ten years ago, I used drugs and alcohol in excess and thought it was OK. Now I am paying for it. And I will still pay a hefty price for it because I will not see my daughter grow up and that makes me sad," Massimo said. He wanted to encourage young Marion to achieve her dream of becoming a professional tennis player. "You may find it difficult to practice every day, to deal with the stress of the matches, and to miss friends' parties," he said, "but everything you do now and the choices you make today will have an impact later. There is no substitute for work. If you want to be a champion, you need to work like a champion today, tomorrow, and every day thereafter."

"At the time, I couldn't really understand why Massimo was so insistent about my future, or why he would not live to see his daughter grow up," Marion said. "But, six months later, he died from HIV, and it was the first time I saw my dad cry."

Shortly thereafter, her father retired as a doctor and began to coach Marion and help her realize her dreams. "He believed I could become a Wimbledon champion. He said it so often that I began to believe it as well, yet I knew it would take a lot of work. We often practiced late into the night. Over the years, my father insisted that we could not end practice until I hit a serve on a target the size of a dinner plate in the far corner of the service square ten times. I did it over and over and over again at very late hours. Even when I was exhausted, I worked and worked and worked because if my coach thought I needed to hit that target, I was going to push through and make it happen."

In 2013, at age 28, Marion won the Wimbledon singles title in straight sets and did not drop a set during the entire tournament. "All those countless hours spent with my father playing on small, sometimes icy, uneven courts had paid off," she told me. "As I stepped up to the line before serving my final ace, I saw my dad in the stands smiling down at me. I whispered, 'Look, Dad,' and then rocked back and served the final point of the match, an ace, in the far corner, just where all those dinner plates had been so many times in practice."

★ Grounding Principle ★

Marion Bartoli didn't stumble accidentally to her Wimbledon title. There was not a magic lightning bolt from the sky. And no one handed it to her. She had a childhood dream of hoisting that fabled trophy someday, and her father's dying patient helped steel her courage to turn that distant vision into a reality. Her dad also kept raising the bar to a Grand Slam level. What Massimo told her years before proved to be absolutely right on: *"Everything you do, every day, will have an impact in the future."*

Lemonade from Lemons

Lemons, in short, don't get turned into lemonade by someone simply looking at them, wanting, and wishing. Someone or something has to do some squeezing to get the process rolling. And no one I know better illustrates this sour-to-sweet continuum than Philadelphia Eagles GM Howie Roseman. In the sports business, there are very few people you can talk to about issues, problems, and opportunities; Howie is one of those people for me and I for him. We have become good friends (and as luck would have it his kids love the 76ers as much as mine love the Eagles). He is one of the good guys—smart, passionate about winning, and 100 percent authentic.

A lot of ten-year-old boys dream of being professional sports stars, doctors, lawyers, and firemen, but when he was that age, Howie had a more specific dream: to be general manager of an NFL team and win a Super Bowl. After graduating from the University of Florida and Fordham Law School, he landed the relatively low-level post of salary-cap staff counsel for the Philadelphia Eagles. A decade later, after working hard, networking, and leveraging his incredible interpersonal skills, Howie (still only 35 years old) emerged as the Eagles' general manager—halfway to his lifelong goal. To secure the other half, Howie and Eagles chairman and CEO Jeffrey Lurie hired a new coach, Chip Kelly.

At first, the move looked brilliant. The Eagles had amassed a woeful 4–12 record in 2012. The next season, the team won ten games and scored a division championship, quite the turnaround. But trouble was brewing. As with most GMs, Roseman oversaw the Eagles' college and pro scouting departments along with the team's medical, equipment, and video staff, while also controlling the team's salary cap and supervising security. But Kelly wanted more control, more power, and freedom from the checks and balances that exist in most successful NFL teams, just like he had at the college level, where he'd built an incredible track record of success.

The job of general manager is one of the most coveted, competitive, and highly scrutinized in the country, and there are only 32 NFL GMs in the world. Howie says, "I always knew I'd lose my job one day. I even told this to Jeffrey Lurie. Because when you're as confident and reliant on analytics as I am, contemplating your eventual unemployment is less a sign of pessimism and more a scientific certainty."

On January 2, 2015, Chip Kelly convinced Lurie to move Howie Roseman from GM to the lesser position of executive vice president of football operations. This was a very public demotion, and it was not easy for Howie to accept. In his new role, Howie continued directing contract negotiations, managing the team's salary cap, and overseeing the team's medical staff, equipment staff, and more, but it was not the same as having all the keys. Lurie, though, was transparent and able to convince Howie to stay with the organization and be patient. Kelly, he argued, would either be the next Bill Belichick, the famously successful then-five-time Super Bowl champion, or not.

What changed for Howie? Well, he lost his seat atop the decision-making tree and was relegated and demoted. He even moved to a smaller office around the corner from his old, down the stairs from the power base of the organization. His responsibilities changed as he lost direct reports over assembling the team. What did not change was his passion to win a Super Bowl and his commitment to the process of being the best version of himself. Sitting in his office, he realized that this might be his last chance to adjust tactics and enrich his perspective while still with the Eagles. What was holding him back? Should he be bolder? Were there new technologies, systems, processes he could learn and adopt? He had two choices: mope around, accept his well-paid but underutilized position, and mail it in, or Trust a Process of his own. A Process where he would commit to learning how to come back and win at the highest level.

When your job is to build a team, insight on how other people do the same is invaluable. "I wanted to broaden my understanding of how other organizations prioritized their operations, from the hiring of people to the timing of announcements," Howie says. "So with the blessing of my boss, I took what I've come to call my 'gap year.' I traveled to London. I went to Manchester City and toured the Aon Training Complex. I spoke at conferences. While I was not sure how long I would still be with the Eagles, it was a calling card I would leverage to meet world-class executives in front offices of the Oklahoma City Thunder, San Antonio Spurs, Chicago Blackhawks, Texas Rangers, L.A. Dodgers, and even

Premier League teams. In addition, I searched beyond the conventional sports-industry Rolodex, spending a day with a Fortune 500 CEO, Frank Bisignano of Fiserv. I listened and learned and absorbed each meeting with exhilarated interest. I was growing as an executive, evaluating where I needed to improve, and preparing for my next step." Back in Philadelphia, Howie sent over one hundred invitations to an information-sharing summit to a diverse group of sports executives from across the industry—team CEOs, presidents, general managers, COOs, coaches—from some of the most innovative teams and sports properties. I was fortunate to be part of this summit. Typically a minute-by-minute planner, Howie outlined the agenda and then facilitated it for the industry leaders as they brainstormed and engaged.

"I was refreshed, I was reinvigorated. I felt fearless and empowered to trust my gut and to trust the people I'd selected to run our organization and play in our colors," he says. All he needed now was an opportunity.

★ Grounding Principle ★

Rather than dwelling negatively about his on-again off-again situation, Howie took the long view. He made the best of his short-term situation but set his sights on the future. He Trusted the Process of self-discovery. And guess what? It worked! As things turned out, Chip

Kelly was in over his head. He very quickly dismantled the team, made a series of bad trades, released star players, and created a culture of mistrust and distrust that eventually ended in his dismissal. In 2016, Howie returned as GM. *He came back smarter, more confident, and ready to take on any challenge, because he committed to his Process and patiently, yet doggedly, spent the necessary time to learn and grow.* Howie quickly rebuilt the roster through a series of shrewd decisions and widely acclaimed draft moves and choices, and a short two years later he looked on with pride as Doug Pedersen coached an underdog Philadelphia Eagles team to a Super Bowl victory over the New England Patriots. The second half of ten-year-old Howie's dream became a reality. Lemonade never tasted better.

Stay the Course—Moving Ahead
Piece by Piece

I first met film director and producer M. Night Shyamalan while doing a radio telethon to raise money for the homeless of Philadelphia. Today, he is a friend and huge 76ers fan who can be seen at most games (when he isn't shooting a film) in the front row next to the visitors' bench.

As he rose up the ranks and became a renowned Hollywood writer, director, and producer, he had the world at his fingertips. Or so it seemed. Despite his status in the industry after a few box-office hits, Night found himself writing things that other people wanted and producing movies that weren't his style thanks to the allure of bigger budgets, exploring different genres, and A-list actors. "I created for others. Sometimes the purpose was honest—a children's film for my children. Other times the temptation to break a record or manage a massive budget was too strong. So with genuine and occasionally disingenuous goals, I created for other people—my children, my studio, my agent, the talent, the public. The wanting to belong and achieve ambition in the wrong way obfuscated my source of power," Night explains. "It wasn't me. I was worthless." Well . . . "worthless" might be a bit strong, at least to those of us who love his movies, but I understand his sentiment. He was not being true to *himself*.

Night was ready to get back to his roots, and he wanted to do it his way. His goal was to quietly make a small, distinctive movie called *The Visit*, which he financed by mortgaging his house. After he and his crew had wrapped production, Night shopped the movie in Hollywood. While he had never shown a first cut to studios, the anxiety and pressure of a self-financed production was too much, and he hoped to identify a studio buyer in advance. Twenty studios saw the rough cut; twenty studios passed. "I boarded the plane home completely shaken. Visions of my self-inflicted financial ruin spiraled in my mind," Night told me. "Moreover, my confidence in my artistic voice was completely shot. I'd had such a pure, clear instinct about this film—and it was wrong. Nobody believed in it. I was lost and powerless." Night has one of the most creative minds in the world, and he was having a crisis of confidence. Knowing this should make us all feel a little bit better when we are struggling, because even the most creative voices of our time struggle. This happens to all of us, but Night discovered the power and importance of Trusting his Process from an unusual inspiration.

Arriving home from that trip, Night closed the front door behind him, happy for just a moment to be safe in the vacuum of his house. His daughter greeted him from the kitchen table, where she was working on a 1,000-piece jigsaw puzzle. "I threw myself into the simplistic and concrete distraction of the puzzle—until we couldn't find a crucial piece we needed to move on. We searched and searched and searched, and kept coming up empty," Night says. We have all been there and know it can be maddening. Night and his daughter sat in silence for what seemed like an hour, Trusting the Process and putting all of their energy into the task of finding that elusive piece. Then there was the most magical moment: they found it. Then they found the next one, then the next one, then the next one. "Just as the puzzle fell into place for us, everything clicked," Night says, the insight seeming crystal clear to him at the time. "Stop looking at the big picture, start with one piece. What if I could do that with *The Visit?*"

★ Grounding Principle ★

The next morning, Night focused on one tiny scene of his movie, editing, considering new vantage points, and reviewing rejected scene takes. "By the end of the day, I had improved that one scene dramatically. The next day I did the same with another scene. The following day another scene. Piece by piece, bit by bit, I kept going until I could see the big picture," Night explained. Three months later, he flew to Hollywood once again and showed the film to the one studio that had invited him for a second showing. They bought it instantly. Universal Pictures in partnership with Night went on to make the movie together, a film that grossed over $300 million (and caused a few sleepless nights for me because I'm terrified of scary movies).

Oftentimes, our challenges do not require a huge makeover or dramatic leap, but small, specific steps in the direction of who we know our best self to be. The future is always movable if you allow yourself to start on the path of where you want to go, and success is often much closer than you think.

Have I Told You Lately That
I Love You?

A few years ago, I went on another father/daughter Young Presidents Organization (YPO) trip, this time with my youngest daughter, Eliza, in the Colorado mountains. She was 11 years old, and when I told her we were going, I didn't get the squeals of excitement that I was expecting. In fact it was the opposite: pure resistance and dread. Eliza is introverted, does not like change, and feels anxious about new experiences. She was feeling a heavy dose of anxiety about the weekend. In the months between me signing us up and the date of the trip, she went from "I don't want to go" to "I won't go" to "If you make me go, I will just stay in the room."

Although the flight to Colorado was amazing (and I lost at so many games of Uno it was mind-numbing), it wasn't quite as enjoyable when we arrived at the camp. As her anxiety around new people and uncertainty began to spike, Eliza opted out of horseback riding, which frustrated me to no end, and she knew it. She tried the same with the 1,500-foot zip line, but I somewhat forced her to do it (not my best dad moment, as I pretty much dragged her up there), and to her credit, she did it and loved it. She tried to get out of the whitewater rafting trip too, but after some tears she got in her wet suit, and, other than a brief moment when she was three inches from the glacier-cold water and saved by our guide, it was a success, and she loved that too. We were connecting in the father-daughter communication classes as well. We were talking about real issues. I was listening more. She was talking more. We were engaging on a whole different level thanks to our facilitator, Dr. Karyn Gordon. On the last day, she served up a final exercise. I was confident that I was ready . . . until I wasn't. The seemingly simple task was not something I had ever thought about.

"Take 30 minutes to write each other a love letter," Dr. Karyn said. "Then go and find a quiet place and read them to each other." Over the years, I had written Eliza hundreds of notes that I put in her lunchbox, left on her pillow, and stuck in her suitcase to tell her I loved her, but this was different and felt more meaningful than a Post-it note. The opportunity to express my feelings and for her to do it to me in writing seemed to weigh on me. I literally cried writing my first sentence because I was so happy to articulate what I know to be true but had not said to her. As we boarded the plane home, Eliza stopped me on the Jetway, leaned in, and gave me a long hug. "Dad, this was the best weekend of my life," she said. "I love you." Given the way we started the trip, that seemed like quite a recovery, and I believe the letter-writing exercise had a lot to do with it.

Here are our love letters. To say it was a powerful assignment is an understatement.

Eliza's Letter to Me:

Dear Dad,

I think you are very brave. You are always trying to be a leader. You are a risktaker. You're charming, energetic, faithful, smart, open-minded, patient, peaceful, and appreciative. When at work, home, or play, you're hardworking. When you did something accidental, I appreciate how honest you are. Your words are gentle and touching. This is the most fun weekend I've ever had! You help me when I am needy. You are playful always! (Except at sleep!) Your rules are always fair. Everything you do has time and effort put into it. I hope you know how much I look up to you and love you. You're very cheerful and outgoing. You're joyful. All the things you plan are organized. I love how passionate you are with things you like. (Once again!) You are a leader. You are a big part of my life. You make my life special. You're very hopeful and humble. I appreciate you more than anything in the world. I hope you always know how much I love you. You are amazing!

Rhinocorns,
Eliza O'Neil

My Letter to Eliza

Eliza—

I love you with all my heart and all my soul. You make this family of ours complete and special. There are so many things I appreciate about you, I hope I can represent some of them to at least capture a piece of how incredible you are and the positive impact you have on me and those that you touch.

You are sensitive. You "feel." You have the gift of emotion. You can sense when others need a hug. You appreciate the special moments in life.

You are creative. You see the world in your own way. You can draw, paint, play, think, stretch, and create in a way that I haven't seen before. The world is yours to create and your canvas to paint to discover the world you will experience, and that will be fun.

You have a strong faith. You believe. You study scriptures. You understand the power that comes with believing in something bigger than you. You understand God's plan and your opportunity. What a blessing.

You are funny. This will serve you well. Oftentimes in life you will have the choice to either laugh or cry, and the more you choose to laugh, bring joy, and make people laugh, it will bring more happiness into the world.

You are confident. You know who you are, and that matters. You understand and accept the responsibility of your gifts.

You are hardworking. You know what has to be done with school and you do it. We don't ask you about homework or studying for a test or a big project because you have decided you will be a great student and you understand the work necessary. This foundation of hard work is an O'Neil trait that you embrace.

You are curious. What an incredible gift this is. You like to learn. You ask a lot of questions. You are observant. You connect the dots and know that life will be changing, and the more you fall in love with learning and growing, the more you will adapt to the changing world. This will serve you well.

You are organized. You know where things go. You like things in their place.

You are generous. Whether it is to help the rhinos or kids who need help and are less fortunate. You always work for those that could use the help. This makes me proud.

You are entrepreneurial. I love watching you explore business ideas and set up art shows. If you choose to start a business, you will be unstoppable.

You love family. Your unconditional love of me, Mom, and Alexa and Kira makes us go as a family. You make us one.

I love you and could write 10 pages of all you are, all your gifts, and the incredible young woman you are.

The world is yours.

Love,
Dad

I know what you're thinking. You don't have the time or inclination to go on a retreat, right? But that's not the point, because you can do something meaningful if you can just stop the hamster wheel you are on for fifteen minutes. Try it. Sit down once a week or once a month with your family and say, "Today we're going to write what we love about X," or, "Four ways to strengthen our family and one thing that we can commit to help that path." When we do this at home, my girls may roll their eyes at the beginning of the exercise, but then it takes just three to four minutes, and they get into it. Sure, my kids may grow up and forget the actual content or anything specific, but I think they will remember that we spent the time together doing something meaningful and that family is the center of the world.

There has never been a more underappreciated class of people than moms. Take out your phone right now and text your mom, tell her why you love her and what you appreciate about her. How would your mother feel? How would you feel? What about that childhood friend you haven't seen in years or your first boss who helped you along the way? We can do better here. Sharing appreciation, gratitude, and love will memorialize how you feel and bring joy to a person who matters.

People Will Tell You That You Are Worthless, but Don't Believe Them

It is not just the love letter exercise and the YPO retreat that made me admire Dr. Karyn Gordon; it was her amazing story of overcoming obstacles. Karyn grew up in a loving and supportive home. Right after faith, education was the highest virtue in the Gordon family. Karyn's grandmother became a medical doctor in the 1940s during the war when she herself was in her forties. (And that was her *second* career.) Her father completed his doctorate at Princeton, and her mother was trained as a teacher, earned a master's in counseling in her fifties, started a second thriving career, and retired in her seventies. Karyn's older sister and brother are both gifted, and both flourished in school.

But learning wasn't easy for Karyn. When she was in school, she worked hard in all her classes, but her grades were still low. Her parents knew something was wrong, and so did Karyn. Finally, when she was 13 years old Karyn's parents had her tested by an educational consultant. "You have a learning disability," the consultant told her after a battery of tests. "To be honest, you'll probably never finish high school." Wait, what? Did he really say that to a seventh-grader? Can you imagine someone saying that to you? To your child? Could you imagine what that would do to a person's drive, confidence, and will to succeed?

At that moment, Karyn's heart sank, her hands started to sweat, and she visualized all her goals and dreams going up in smoke. "I had no idea at the time how this experience would change my life. Fortunately, it was not the verdict the consultant delivered, but how my parents responded," she says. "That became my most valuable lesson."

From that day forward, Karyn's parents said they would never ask to see her report card, something that shocked her. After all, they were the hard-charging, we-get-straight-A's-in-this-house kind of parents. "We know you can't control your marks, but you can control your effort 100 percent. So instead, when it's report card day, we will have one simple question for you: Did you try your absolute best?" her father said. "You can control this, so we will hold you accountable to that standard." The Process is what they were going to measure and track.

"This unique parenting approach wouldn't work for every child, but my parents knew how to inspire and reach me. In that moment, my dad's words generated a powerful movement of hope and intrinsic motivation within me," Karyn explains.

It turns out, her father was right. Karyn was committed and driven to follow this Process and control her effort and time management. She would try to understand her learning disability, ask for help, see tutors, talk with her teachers, and build solid self-discipline and study habits. The more she focused on her own progress, the more hopeful and motivated she became. Thankfully, that translated into higher marks. Despite what the consultant said, Karyn went to college and eventually got her doctorate. Yes, you are reading that correctly, her *PhD*. "That happened for two reasons only: first, I was willing to work insanely hard; more importantly, my parents' philosophy inspired me to place all my focus on what I *can* control instead of comparing myself to others," she explains.

★ Grounding Principle ★

In an era when we see epidemic rates of anxiety among young people and employees in America, one of the greatest lessons Karyn teaches within both organizational and family systems is this: hold people accountable for what they can control. When individuals become empowered by this message, they learn to focus on the right things (their thoughts and actions), and anxiety evaporates. "Looking back to when I was 13, I had no idea that such a powerful lesson would come out of a life circumstance that was so painful. I saw my learning disability as a curse, but today I recognize it as one of my greatest gifts. It taught me how to connect and teach in a way that reaches more people," Karyn says. *This process showed her the importance of seeking wise counsel and surrounding herself with people who would help her achieve her goals.* When I heard this story, it taught me that life is truly a journey, full of powerful lessons, if only we stop to listen to those who love us enough to challenge us, provide us with feedback along the way, and continue to build us up.

Your Turn to Put This into Practice

Most of us need to do a better job communicating with each other and sharing our feelings. Think of someone you love. Imagine you had only one hour with this person for the rest of your life. This could be a spouse, parent, friend, or partner. Write down what you would tell that person, and then put it in an envelope and send it.

Epilogue

I would like to end with a quote from John Gardner, professor of public service in the Graduate School of Business at Stanford University, from an article called "Rewind Your Clock." It has stayed with me since my mom shared it decades ago.

Meaning is not something you stumble across . . . Meaning is something you build into your life. You build it out of your own past, out of your affections and loyalties, out of the experience of humankind as it is passed on to you out of your own talent and understanding, out of the things and people you love, out of the values for which you are willing to sacrifice something. The ingredients are there. You are the only one who can put them together into that unique pattern that will be your life. Let it be a life that has dignity and meaning for you. If it does, then the particular balance of success or failure is of less account.
—John Gardner

ACKNOWLEDGMENTS

My life has been blessed with an unmatched village of mentors, teachers, coaches, friends, family, bosses, and coworkers who are simply the most inspiring people in the world. Thank you to all who have shaped me, my life, and my perspective—*Be Where Your Feet Are* is my attempt to share some of the lessons you've taught me; it represents the way I aspire to walk through the world. I wish I could name you all, but if I did, that would be a book unto itself.

Be Where Your Feet Are is not written, published, or gracing the digital shelves of readers across the world without the following forces of nature:

Tim Bartlett. You are simply amazing. I appreciate your diligence, your push to make this book great, your edits, direction, guidance, and friendship . . . and of course your fandom of the 76ers. As a first-time author, I recognize how fortunate I am to work with you, but maybe even more fortunate to call you a guide and friend. Additionally, from St. Martin's Press, I'd like to thank Joel Fotinos, founder of the

Essentials imprint, who understood my intentions (and appreciated my naiveté) immediately and provided wise counsel from the ideation and framing stages to the final copy. Assistant Editor Alice Pfeifer handled details large and small with aplomb. Associate Publisher Anne Marie Tallberg was an early and strong supporter of the book. Cover Designer Young Lim crushed it. The team of Brant Janeway, VP of Marketing, and John Karle, Associate Director of Publicity, have been incredible partners. Copy Editor Ryan Masteller gave the book an extra layer of polish for which I am grateful. Managing Editor Alan Bradshaw kept the book on schedule with professionalism, courtesy, and calm. An additional thank-you goes to Laury Frieber for her legal feedback.

Jan Miller, extraordinary agent to the stars (and me)—the opportunity to work alongside you and learn from the best in the world has been a gift. I am forever indebted to you and inspired by your spirit, determination, drive, and willingness to show up fully present. You bring joy to the grind.

Randal Wright—you have been a North Star for me and Lisa. Your lessons, lectures, books, and stories are brilliant, moving, and purposeful. Your friendship, guidance, and encouragement delivered this book. We began this journey together, and I am proud the sibling books we have created share a foundation and core. You are a spiritual giant whose love of others has made an indelible mark on the world. And, yes, I will three-word-journal this experience.

Michele Bender—you are a true talent and an even better person, mom, and friend. Thank you for moving my 115 mph mind onto the page. From our shared love of learning to your tireless, dogged determination, you truly willed this book into existence. I could not imagine writing this book with anyone else, and I thank you for always showing up as your authentic self.

Lara Toscani Weems—you are a force of nature—a super mom, super writer, and super editor. Your insights, suggestions, and edits helped me weave this book together from the very beginning. Thank you for repeatedly reading, and rereading, all the early drafts, offering critiques, and standing by me while I developed my writing process.

Elizabeth Forster—your dedication and countless hours poured into keeping this book on track have been invaluable. You are smart, driven, and passionate, and I feel fortunate to work with you so early in what I am confident will become a long, truly special, career.

Denise Krieg—you have been by my side since the start of my career and have been an incredible source of support for me. There is simply no one in the industry who manages the way you do—simply put: you are infamous, in the best way.

Jon Liebman. You have many incredible gifts—I

continue to be impressed by your instinct-guided leadership style.

Stacy O'Neil. My sister-in-law, world-beating talent executive, entrepreneur, and producer. Thank you for advising, shepherding, and steering me to a truly brilliant team of executives. You continue to light the world on fire.

Mark Fortier and Meg Cassidy of Fortier Public Relations. Thank you for believing in this project. Your passion, coaching, relationships, and experience allowed the book to meet its opportunity.

Family, family, family.

Lisa, you are a source of strength, light, and happiness. I love you and appreciate every second we have together. Your commitment to family, your steadfast faith, and your lifelong commitment to learning make me grateful everyday knowing we will be together forever. Alexa, thank you for bringing light, life, and energy into every room you enter. Kira, thank you for your kindness, brilliance, and empathetic heart; you shine. Eliza, thank you for feeling, seeing, and loving at an unmatched level; while I have always been your coach, you have taught me so much more than I could ever teach you. The gifts the four of you possess will impact the world in which you play; so play on the biggest court you can find. Never forget that you are my WMI. I love you all with all of my heart.

The O'Neil family—Thank you for your unshakable faith in me and for always believing in me and cheering me on in every endeavor. I am so unbelievably fortunate to be able to rely on all of you for endless advice, support, and comic relief. You have stood by me and have been my greatest advocates. Mom—for teaching me how to work unreasonably hard, root for others, and tell stories. I love you, appreciate you, and thank you for shaping my perspective on the world. Doc—for teaching me to have a competitive fire and convincing me I could be anything I wanted to be. Sean—for making me tough and stretching me past my comfort zone. Erin, Matt, Ryan, Julia, Olivia, Michael—for picking me up when I fall and lifting me higher as you climb. Wendy, Calla, Ava, Matthew—for teaching me unconditional love. Jenny, Harry, Mae, Wil, Shannon—for making me laugh and showing me what a superhero is. And Trey—thank you for the laughs, love, and reminders that the roller-coaster of life is the best teacher.

The Reynolds family— thank you for the focus on family, the reinforcement that life is better together and to meet people where they are in life. I appreciate laughing and crying together, and bringing the Sunday dinner back into fashion. This family is a circle of strength and love. Mom (Janet), Dad (Dee), Jason, Steph, Josh, McCall, Jeremy, Tara, Kim, Steve, Isaak, Ben, Addi, Ashley, Teag, Dallas, Greyson, Emily,

Makenzie, Katelyn, Harper, Jake— for being you and bringing your authentic selves everywhere you go. It has been the gift of a lifetime working with and learning from you. There is nobody I have ever come across who is better at identifying and developing talent and building a world-class culture than you.

The Cardon family—I love you. Wil—I miss you. Nicole—you are the strength we need in this world. Rebecca, Bo, Parley, Ruby, and Scarlett—continue to see the light and be the light in the world. You are the gifts that keep on giving.

The incredible fans of the (then) New Jersey Nets, Philadelphia Eagles, New York Knicks, New York Rangers, New York Liberty, Philadelphia 76ers, New Jersey Devils, Dignitas, 76ers Gaming Club, and so many others. Your passion, fandom, and support challenge me each day to be the most innovative and impactful executive I can be—and for that I am forever grateful. (And if I blocked you on Twitter, it is because my kids follow me too, and some language simply is not appropriate.) I am grateful for the standing ovation, roar of the crowd, and the way you lift a player and a team when it counts the most. Sports is the most powerful vehicle in the world to bring people together, and I have witnessed its awesome power around the world, and that gives meaning and purpose to what we do.

To the GMs, coaches, and players I have had the privilege to watch, cheer on, and get to know. Greatness, brilliance, and excellence are never an accident—I wish more people saw how hard you have to work to make it look so easy. Thank you.

My fellow NBA and NHL team presidents and CEOs. Very few people will ever know and understand the pressure, long hours, and intensity of our jobs. You are simply the best in the world at what you do—leading and inspiring front offices, athletes, and communities alike—and I am honored to call you friends: Steve Koonin, Rich Gotham, John Abbamondi, Fred Whitfield, Michael Reinsdorf, Nic Barlage, Len Komoroski, Cynthia Marshall, Matt Hutchings, Josh Kroenke, Arn Tellem, Rick Welts, Tad Brown, Rick Fuson, Gillian Zucker, Tim Harris, Jason Wexler, Eric Woolworth, Peter Feigin, Ethan Casson, Dennis Lauscha, Kristin Bernert, Dave Hopkinson, Andy Lustgarten, Danny Barth, Charlie Freeman, Alex Martins, Jason Rowley, Chris McGowan, Matina Kolokotronis, John Rinehart, R. C. Buford, Michael Friisdahl, Jim Olson, Jim Van Stone, Don Waddell, Michael Priest, Lou Lamoriello, John Davidson, Chuck Fletcher, David Morehouse, Dick Patrick, Cam Neely, Kim Pegula, Christopher Ilitch, Chris Granger, Rory Babich, Geoff Molson, France Margaret Belanger, Steve Griggs, Brendan Shanahan, Anthony LeBlanc, Danny Wirtz, Jim Lites, Matt Majka, David Poile, Doug Armstrong, John Olfert, Michael Schulman, Xavier Gutierrez, Ken King, Bob Nicholson, Luc Robitaille,

Jonathan Becher, Michael Doyle, Kerry Bubolz, and Dan Beckerman.

To the hundreds of front-office employees at the Philadelphia 76ers, New Jersey Devils, and all of the Sixers Innovation Lab and HBSE Ventures entrepreneurs. I am honored, humbled, happy, and appreciative to get to wake up every day and sprint to work next to you.

The managing and limited partners at Harris Blitzer Sports & Entertainment: Josh Harris, David Blitzer, Michael Rubin, Rodger Krouse, Marc Leder, Marty Geller, James Lassiter, Adam Aron, Will Smith, and Brad Krouse. Thank you for the infinite guidance you have given me and for the opportunity to run the greatest franchise in all of sports and entertainment; build the most innovative and diverse workforce in the industry; create true, palpable, positive change in the communities we serve; and inspire an audience of global sports fans across the world. It is truly a blessing to be able to work with each of you.

I have had the pleasure of learning from and in some cases working for and alongside some of the most talented individuals on the planet, and without all of you, I would not be where, or who, I am today. You all have allowed me to lead and be led. Thank you for believing in me and guiding me along my journey. A few of my many influential former, and some present, friends, colleagues, and bosses: Jeff Lurie, Joe

Banner, Jon Spoelstra, David Stern, Adam Silver, Arnie Prives, Bruce Schilling, Giovanni Mazzarelli, Jim Walker, Jeff Piluso, Mike Addeo, Jim Loricchio, Bernie Mullin, John Larkin, Ron Skotarczak, Travis Williams, Eric Hinds, Matt Kelly, Buck Holmes, Steve Vitale, Brian Blair, Scott Cutler, Ben Sibbett, David Young, Chester Elton, Howie Nuchow, Mike Levine, Paul Danforth, Scott Storck, Brett Yormark, Jeff Auerbach, Karen Levine, Chad Estis, Mike Ondrejko, John Cudmore, Mark Piazza, Seth Berger, Adam Kanner, Jared Stone, Chris Dodge, Jon Hawkins, Greg Davis, Geoff Brown, Tagg Romney, Drew Johnson, Roger Morgan, Toby Shorter, Mike Antinoro, Peter Horn, Shelby Christensen, Amber Skoubye, Daniel Skoubye, Daniel Daniel, Jimmy Dunn, Sam Evans, Tanya Curry, Steve Ross, Russ Dalby, Leo Carlin, Natasha Eno, Jeffrey Smith, Jim Fox, Steve Castleton, Matt Eyring, Spencer Holt, who taught me that small things make a big difference, Karl Fails, Dan Ware, Mateo Furner, Jason Nusca, Russell M. Nelson, Paul Brown, Steve Starks, Ryan Smith, Doc Rivers, Sam Hinkie, Ray Shero, Donnie Walsh, Kirsten Corio, Glen Grunwald, Brett Brown, Mike D'Antoni, Colin Neville, Alex Michael, Harold Cho, Akshay Khanna, Jason Robbins, Jim Kenney, Patrick Murphy, Phil Murphy, Darren Rovell, Stephanie Ruhle, Scott Soshnick, Kevin Negandhi, Kevin Arnovitz, Jeff Zillgitt, Maria Bartiromo, Amy Jo Martin, Morgan Jones, Stephen

A. Smith, Mike Missanelli, Anthony Gargano, Abe Madkour, John Lombardo, Terry Lefton, Jimmy Worrall, James Emmett, Elliotte Friedman, Eric Chemi, Graeme Roustan, Ukee Washington, Alaa Abdelnaby, Marc Zumoff, Ken Daneyko, Howard Beck, Christina Alesci, Greg Wyshnyski, Tom Moore, Keith Pompey, John George, Darren Heitner, Joe DeCamara, Jamie Lynch, Bob Cooney, John Gonzalez, Mike Jerrick, Alex Holley, Quincy Harris, Sharrie Williams, Jamie Apody, Chris Kaufman, Casey Coffman, Daryl Morey, Howard Jacobs, Elton Brand, Tom Fitzgerald, Lindy Ruff, Bryan Colangelo, Adam Davis, Jake Reynolds, Chris Heck, Hugh Weber, Brad Shron, David Collins, David Abrams, Elizabeth Berman, Gabe Harris, Katie O'Reilly, Jonathan Fascitelli, Dave Sholler, Andy Aninsman, Marty Capasso, Milan Kunz, Bruce Winn, Kenny Lower, John Hutchinson, Corbin Walburger, Dave Checketts, Morgan Jones, Brian Adams, Bryan Bunker, Lara Price, Susan Williamson, Dr. Aimee Kimball, Sean Saadeh, Brittanie Boyd, David Gould, Ian Hillman, Jillian Frechette, Dana Seiden, Rob Newson, Brian Norman, Ben Cobleigh, Jill Snodgrass, Natasha Moody, Dave Reid, Dan MacKinnon, Nicole Armellino, Pete Albietz, Paul DiCicco, World B. Free, Sonny Hill, Evan Zemsky, Isaac Harrouche, Joel Karansky, Clayton Witta, Brandon Moss, Gary Bettman, Bill Daly, Keith Wachtel, Mark Tatum,

Bill Sutton, Adam Silver, Jim Dolan, Danny Meiseles, Sandy Montag, Sumeet Goel, Tie Domi, Jordan Bazant, Michael Neuman, Jay Marciano, Alan Ostfield, Paul Speaker, Peter Farnsworth, Jim Esposito, Sophie Goldschmidt, Jim Ferrell, Bill McDermott, Chad Lewis, Casey Wasserman, SamD Kennedy, Jeff Gorton, Howie Roseman, Mike D'Antoni, Donnie Walsh, Adam Grant, Glen Sather, John Tortorella, Tom Renney, Brian Rolapp, Rob Manfred, Dan Reed, Tom Glick, Amy Brooks, Irwin Simon, Gracie Mercado, Stacy McWilliams, Donna Daniels, David Ware, Clark Maxwell, Vai Sikahema, and the O'Bats family.

The Young Presidents Organization (YPO) forum crew: Henry Johnson, Ben Feder, Alex Farman-Farmaian, Safi Bahcall, Greg Warner, Will Margiloff, Sheldon Lehman. You all have taught me more about life, love, and the pursuit of happiness than I can even begin to articulate. Your friendship, passion, creativity, hard work, and sacrifice are inspiring. You are amazing leaders and even better people. Thank you.

My fellow Elevate Sports Ventures partners: Al Guido, Jed York, Tim Leiweke, Irving Azoff, Jared Smith, Michael Rapino, Chip Bowers, Sean Kundu, Shawn Doss, Flavil Hampsten, Jeff Knapple, and Moon Javaid. I am proud and fortunate to be able to work with executives and longtime friends whom I admire and respect as much as you all. Thank you for your drive and determination to transform the sports and entertainment industry.

The storytellers: Thank you to all of the friends, family, colleagues, and executives who took the time and effort to send me stories, personal experiences, and life lessons as I began writing this book. These intimate pieces of your lives that you vulnerably shared have helped shape this book and helped me learn and grow. Thank you for your wisdom and inspiration throughout the writing process. You have made this book possible, and I am truly grateful. And, no, I did not use all of the stories, as that would have been impossible, but your stories influenced my writing, guided me to the principles, and enriched my life, and for that I am forever grateful. They include: David Adelman, Kenny Albert, Bandar bin Muhammed Al-Saud, Christopher Anderson, Crystal Barkley, Phineas Barnes, Marion Bartoli, Jordan Bazant, Craig Bench, Murray Benyon, Seth Berger, Jack Birch, Brian Blair, Darren Bonnstetter, Dee Bostic, Sid Brown, Sarah Bua, Libby Bush, James Cash, AJ Cass, Ethan Casson, Vincent Chan, Murray Cohn, Pat Croce, Melissa Cutler, Scott Cutler, Paul Danforth, Ryan Davenport, Greg Davis, Chris Dodge, Jamie Doffermyre, Tie Domi, John Doherty, Desron Dorset, Shawn Doss, Chester Elton, David Esposito, Jacques Henri Eyraud, Ben Feder, Jim Ferrell, Jim Fiore, Mark Fischer, Scott Fisher, Lesa Kennedy France, Chris Gaffney, Don Garber, Jessica Gelman,

Karyn Gordon, Rich Gotham, Andrea Greenberg, Shaun Greene, Lorin Gresser, Al Guido, Sunil Gulati, Michael Guth, Lindsay Harding, Rick Haring, Dan Harris, Rick Heitzmann, Jerome Heppelmann, Steven Herbst, Eric Hinds, Rich Hill, Sonny Hill, Scott Hillboe, Lara Hodgson, Karen Hung, Brandon Ingersoll, Don Jabro, Conn Jackson, Mark Jackson, Sean Jacobsohn, Brett Jewkes, Henry Johnson, Archie Jones, Adam Kanner, John Keenan, Dave Kelleher, Jonathan Kemp, Tim Kemp, Sam Kennedy, Ben King, Laurence Knight, Steve Koonin, Denise Krieg, John Larkin, Joe Leccese, Emuh Leet, Tim Leiweke, Jim Leonard, Mike Levinthal, David Levy, Max Liechtenstein, Greg Loewen, Jim Loricchio, Kenny Lower, Melissa Lower, Marc Lucenius, Abe Madkour, Walter Maloney, Bill Manning, Shannon Mannon, Amy Jo Martin, Clark Maxwell, Antonio Mazzarelli, Steve McClatchy, Kevin McCormick, Bill McDermott, Patrick McGinn, Dan McGuiggan, Brandt McKee, Kane McLaughlin, Sean McManus, Carole McNaughton, Kim McNaughton, Stacy McWilliams, Gracie Mercado, David Merritt, Alex Michael, Shervin Mirhashemi, Junior Moyo, Tricia Naddaff, Miles Nadal, Shawn Nelson, Michael Neuman, Howie Nuchow, Lou O'Neil, Matt O'Neil, Mary Ann O'Neil, Michael O'Neil, Sean O'Neil, Shannon O'Neil, Wendy O'Neil, Melissa Ormond, Nicole Pawlak, Joseph Perrello, Jeff Piluso, Sarah Premo, Lara Price, Paul Rabil, Peter Reinhardt, Emily Reynolds,

Jake Reynolds, Jason Reynolds, McCall Reynolds, Steph Reynolds, Dan Rice, Wendy Richards, Ari Roitman, Tagg Romney, Howie Roseman, Scott Rosner, Nicole Russell, Heb Ryan, Patrick Ryan, Brian Santiago, Sunny Sanyal, Adrianne Shapira, Alex Sheen, Jeff Shifrin, Dave Sholler, M. Night Shyamalan, Vai Sikahema, Eric Simon, Darnell Smith, Jill Snodgrass, Jaime Smith, Jerry Solomon, Bob Sommer, Lily Song, Scott Sonnenberg, Scott Soshnick, Brandon Steiner, Susan Steiner, David Stern, Rick Stockton, Harlan Stone, Jared Stone, Bill Sutton, Rahim Thompson, Scott Thomson, Tony Thornton, Craig Turnbull, Q Turner, Troy Tutt, Nada Usina, Jim Walker, Chris Wallace, Chris Wallis, Greg Warner, Marquise Watson, Hugh Weber, Chris Weil, Fred Whitfield, Whitney Williams, Matthew Wood, Eric Woolworth, Brett Yormark, David Young, Sheela Goud Zemlin.

Early endorsements came in from a who's who of bestselling authors and world-class people: Adam Grant, Angela Duckworth, Chester Elton, Safi Bahcall, and Kim Scott. Your words of encouragement and feedback made a sometime lonely labor of love fun.

INDEX

ABOUT THE AUTHOR

Alex Subers

SCOTT M. O'NEIL is one of the most respected, connected, and dynamic executives in the sports and entertainment industry. He has more than 25 years of experience leading NBA, NHL, and NFL organizations. This Harvard Business School–educated change agent has built a reputation as an innovative, people-first "leader of leaders." As the CEO of the Philadelphia 76ers and New Jersey Devils, his mission is to build high integrity, uber-talented, inspiring, inclusive, and high-performing teams whose members will become the next generation of great leaders. A decade-long member of the NBA and NHL boards of governors, O'Neil's insights have made him a prominent, regular voice on Bloomberg, FOX Business, CNBC, and CNN. A man of faith, husband, and father of three, O'Neil's conviction to lead a perpetually grounded and present life guides his commitment to helping others realize their full potential. He lives in Pennsylvania with his family. Learn more at scottoneil.com and follow him @ScottONeil.